The Author:

Ernest B. Koenker is professor in the Graduate School of Religion at the University of Southern California. He is the author of THE LITURGICAL RENAISSANCE IN THE ROMAN CATHOLIC CHURCH and WORSHIP IN WORD AND SACRAMENT.

SECULAR SALVATIONS

Secular Salvations

THE RITES AND SYMBOLS OF POLITICAL RELIGIONS

Ernest B. Koenker

FORTRESS PRESS   Philadelphia

Biblical quotations from the Revised Standard Version of the Bible, copyrighted 1946 and 1952 by the Division of Christian Education of the National Council of the Churches of Christ in the United States of America, are used by permission.

© 1965 by FORTRESS PRESS

Library of Congress Catalog Card Number 65-22554

2398C65   Printed in U.S.A.   UB996

To my wife Hazel

and to my children Mark, Deborah, and Gregory

PREFACE

This is a study of the cult of what Spengler foresaw as a "second religiousness." Ours has been the age par excellence of political faiths, of secular salvations offered on a national or universal scale. Intricate new mythologies and rituals have been constructed by these disenchanted believers, and millions more lives have been offered on the altars of these new devotions than were offered in the persecution of Christians in the Roman Empire. Parties have laid claim to men's ultimate devotion. They have elicited a self-sacrificing enthusiasm for an idea or for a corporate reality superior to the mean individual. Men have turned to blind believing in an effort to overcome the emptiness of their lives.

The documentary material included in the text and in the appendices is presented to illustrate specific attempts to construct a civil religion. In one way or another each of these experiments adapts Christian forms to social uses. My thanks are expressed to Dr. Hoch of the Institut für Zeitgeschichte in Munich for material on Nazi festivals, to Dr. Murawski and Dr. von Friesen of the Bundesministerium für gesamtdeutsche Fragen in Bonn for materials and photographs on Communist rites, and to Mrs. Agnes Peterson of the Hoover Institution at Stanford University for interlibrary loan materials. Thanks are also due to Pastor Wilhelm Niemoeller, director of the Archiv der Bekennenden Kirche at Bielefeld, for use of documents from the Archiv. Dr. Oskar Söhngen, vice-president of the Evangelical Church of the Union and author of *Säkularisierter Kultus,* also offered suggestions.

In the preparation of the manuscript Mr. John Strietelmeier, University Editor at Valparaiso University, offered valuable suggestions. I thank my former student aides at Valparaiso University for typing the manuscript, particularly Mrs. Nancy Hauger, Mr. Charles Evanson, and Miss Marilyn Schreiber. I am grateful as well to the many other people who during the last twelve years have offered suggestions and recommended sources utilized here.

ERNEST B. KOENKER

Valparaiso, Indiana
St. Michael and All Angels, 1964

ACKNOWLEDGEMENTS

Grateful acknowledgment is made to the following for permission to quote from the works cited: Allyn and Bacon, *Democracy in America; The Manchester Guardian Weekly,* "America Goes to Church"; Alfred A. Knopf, *The Rebel;* Harper and Row, *The New Shape of American Religion, The Labyrinth, Pagan and Christian Mysteries,* and *Why They Behave Like Russians;* Simon and Schuster, *The Poetry and Prose of Walt Whitman;* United States Information Agency, *Problems of Communism;* The University of Chicago Press, *Systematic Theology;* Oxford University Press, *Education for Death;* Adam Ulam and *The Reporter,* "The Displaced Mummy"; Geoffrey Bles and The University of Michigan Press, *The Origin of Russian Communism;* The Macmillan Company, *Russia in Flux;* National Lutheran Council, *Report to the Evangelical Church in Germany; East Europe,* "Battle for Belief"; Lewis S. Feuer and Doubleday and Company, *Basic Writings on Politics and Philosophy;* Doubleday and Company, *The Eastern Orthodox Church* and *To the Finland Station;* Philosophical Library, *The Perennial Scope of Philosophy;* Harcourt, Brace and World, and Routledge and Kegan Paul, *Ideology and Utopia;* Harcourt, Brace and World, and George Allen and Unwin, *The Origins of Totalitarianism;* Harcourt, Brace and World, *Marxism and Modern Thought;* University of Notre Dame Press, *The Soviet Union;* Hafner Publishing Company, *The Social Contract;* Yale University Press, *The Living and the Dead: A Study of the Symbolic Life of Americans;* William Hodge and Company, *First Commandment;* Beacon Press, *Religion and Philosophy in Germany;* Dr. Oskar Söhngen, *Säkularisierter Kultus;* Gütersloher Verlagshaus Gerd Mohn, *Kirchliches Jahrbuch;* The Ronald Press Company, *The Course of American Political Thought;* Houghton Mifflin Company, *Mein Kampf.*

CONTENTS

1
THE CHRISTIAN
BETWEEN FAITH AND IDEOLOGY

> THE *Americans not only follow their religion from interest, but they often place in this world the interest which makes them follow it. In the Middle Ages the clergy spoke of nothing but a future state; they hardly cared to prove that a sincere Christian may be a happy man here below. But the American preachers are constantly referring to the earth; and it is only with great difficulty that they can divert their attention from it. To touch their congregations, they always show them how favorable religious opinions are to freedom and public tranquility; and it is often difficult to ascertain from their discourses whether the principal object of religion is to procure eternal felicity in the other world or prosperity in this.*
>
> ALEXIS DE TOCQUEVILLE, *Democracy in America* (1840)[1]

In their doctrine, their cult, and their devotion the ideologies represent the great alternatives, the live options, to Christianity in the twentieth century. These ideologies, whether Nazism, Communism, Fascism, or Democracy, again and again have constituted themselves new ecclesiastical and spiritual centers which vie for men's allegiance. Sometimes the struggle may be in our home town or in our own hearts. At other times it involves fellow Christians at vast distances. Usually it involves the young, but sometimes it even catches up with the old, with those on the margins of life. The following note from a pastor in East Germany is a single pathetic instance illustrating a conflict repeated many times:

---

[1] *Democracy in America,* Vol. II, trans. Henry Reeve (Boston: John Allyn, Publisher, 1862). Courtesy of Allyn and Bacon, Inc., Boston.

To: The Church Council of Schwerin [East Germany].

Regarding: Christmas Services in Homes for the Aged.

With reference to the request cited above I must announce that in the Home for the Aged, Schneienstrasse 20a, as was the case last year, a Christmas celebration cannot be held.

In the previous year the District Council had approved a Christmas devotion, but the governess of the home refused permission. When on Second Christmas Day, 1958, I called on ailing Evangelical inmates of the home during regular visiting hours I was turned out by the governess [Frau M.] and by an SED [Socialist Unity Party] functionary she had summoned. Later, at the discussion with the District Council, the governess declared that there was no desire among the inmates for a Christmas devotion or for a pastoral visit.

It is obvious that none of the home's inmates would venture to express such a desire any more. All of them fear the fanatical Christ-hater Frau M. They even fear being "thrown out" or having some trick played on them. An old woman who had to withdraw from the home at Frau M.'s request and transfer to a home in the country was of the opinion that this occurred because of her unflinching attitude toward the church. A married couple requested the celebration of the Lord's Supper, since the wife was very sick. They came to the church, knowing that Frau M. would not permit a house-communion. When the wife died the governess arranged for a Socialist burial service, against the wishes of the husband. It was with difficulty that relatives from out of town were able at the last moment to countermand the Socialist speaker and to request me to give her Christian burial. The widower simply could get nowhere with the governess. Though I was able to bury this woman, still in the case of Frau B., who had no relatives to intercede so decisively, it was impossible; Frau B., a faithful Christian who was always very happy over my visits, received Socialist burial. After all these incidents it is no longer possible to provide spiritual care for the inmates of the home, to say nothing of holding a devotion. So I have made no further attempt to receive permission from the District Council to hold a Christmas devotion. Even if I were given permission, the old people would no longer dare attend.[2]

Behind the Iron Curtain even the corpses of the aged are prized for their usefulness in the Communist rites. Yet it is for the young

[2] *Kirchliches Jahrbuch,* ed. Joachim Beckmann (Gütersloh: Gütersloher Verlagshaus, Gerd Mohn, 1961), pp. 152-53.

that Communism really vies, for the Communist Caesar has great work for them to do. The question faced by most Christians in Eastern Europe is simply whether or not they are to approve and support the requirements of an atheistic state. Their question is one of elementary civil obedience. Most avenues of cultural influence are effectively closed to Christians. Is one to acquiesce to the demands of a professedly godless state? When is one lending support to the "confessional" regime?

In Eastern Europe it is less easy than in America to coast along on a mediocre version of Christian faith. American religiousness is too successful, too optimistic, pragmatic, and activistic to sense accurately the suffering Christianity of Eastern Europe today. One is reminded of Luther's remark, *Ecclesia vera est ecclesia pressa* ("The true church is the suffering church"). In America there is seldom a reproach for bearing the name of Jesus Christ because his name no longer stands for anything specific, either doctrinally or morally. There is more confidence in the right words and in pious routines than in the power of the living God and in the healing Gospel. The god of the majority of Americans is a most usable entity. He guarantees success to our undertakings rather than standing in judgment over them. He promises security rather than enabling us to live, by faith, amid insecurities.

When given such a common religion as "Americanism" it is not surprising that various segments in society use the church for their purposes. The church stabilizes family unity, guards society's welfare, and justifies what the nation wants. God becomes the servant of all the designs and desires of men rather than the judge of their cherished interests.

The Christian Serving God and Caesar

However, the relationship between Christianity and the ideologies is not simply one of mutual exclusion. The Christian endeavors to live his life in faithfulness to the rule of Christ *and* under the *imperium* of state power. There will inevitably be conflicts between these allegiances. St. Augustine saw this conflict in terms of "enjoyment," reserved for God alone, and "use," applicable to all created things in an ordered structure. But he perceived this difference between the earthly and heavenly cities, that "the good use the world that they may enjoy God: the wicked, on the contrary, that they may enjoy the world would fain use God."[3] The modernity of St. Augustine is nowhere more apparent than in the "use" of God on the American scene today.

It is one of the tasks of Christian theology to unmask the subtle idolatries, the pseudo-religions, and pseudo-theologies in each age. The pretensions of Roman Caesarism forced the early Christian apologists to this task. St. Augustine explored the problem in terms of his two militant cities, and repeatedly, in the experience of the church sojourning in the world, the relation of church to world has had to be reexamined and reevaluated. In view of the significance of the claims of the various ideologies the church cannot simply overlook the answers they propose. The Christian understanding of man can be formulated only in continual dialogue with the conceptions of man evident in the ideologies. Through a study of their antithetical rites a more fruitful understanding of the distinctive nature of Christian faith and worship should emerge. Actually, only from the living encounter with these alternatives does the unique genius of the Christian message appear. Only in confrontation with twentieth-century political rites do the Christian rites and sacraments reveal their full dimensions. Through a more complete participation in these dimensions the church may well hope to gain a new capacity to counter the secular rites through worship in Spirit and in truth.

The emergence of such forms as these in highly sophisticated environments is a phenomenon which has received relatively little attention. Anthropologists, psychologists, and sociologists have devoted painstaking studies to symbols and rites in archaic and preliterate cultures, yet the new cultic forms connected with the ideologies have elicited only *aperçus*. But precisely this transition to

[3] *The City of God* (New York: Modern Library, 1950), Bk. XV, Chap. 7, p. 485.

4

cultic forms reveals the thoroughness of the secularization process which has been proceeding apace for centuries in Western culture. While Christian forms, beliefs, and practices have been secularized, the "secular" has become more religious. It is the writer's wish that these chapters may shed some light on the relationship of these rites and symbols to the Christian faith and that they may stimulate further exploration in these areas. The rites examined in the following pages reveal clearly the inner nature of their sponsoring movement. By means of a "theological method" Nazism and Communism, for example, have applied their basic tenets to the conduct of life. Often the strongest moral sentiments, which put Christian morality to shame, have motivated their adherents. The cultural and religious milieu surrounding these rites—the disintegration, the meaninglessness, the new expectations—provide a disturbing picture of the prospects facing Christianity today. Some light may be cast via these rites on the sobering challenge confronting the churches in America, too. The secular rites are no incidental or peripheral phenomenon. They bid actually to displace Christian faith and sacraments.

It should be pointed out that the claims of democracy—and even those of Fascism—have been far less extensive and inclusive than those of consistent totalitarianism. Moreover, because of their restricted claims these ideologies have not proceeded to attack or replace the rites and practices of Christianity in the same explicit fashion as Nazism and Communism have done. The crucial point, however, as pursued in this study, always revolves about the "religious" question of ultimate devotion, on the basis of which, finally, our decisions are made. The many nuances in thought and emphasis, varying interminably from hour to hour and from place to place, may seem not to receive sufficient illumination in this effort to include a comprehensive and comparative picture. For example, in examining Nazism neither the tenets nor the forms of politically-infected Christians should be confused with those of avowed anti-Christians. The efforts of the "German Christians" (*Deutsche Christen*) to achieve a synthesis between National Socialism and

Christianity must be distinguished from the objectives of those Nazi leaders who were committed to the destruction of Christianity. They must be distinguished also from the goals of the *Duetsche Glaubensbewegung,* from those of Ludendorff's *Tannenburg Bund,* from Hitler's National Socialist Party, from those of the SS. Again, the techniques of the Communist Party in Poland differ radically from the techniques in the U.S.S.R. and in East Germany. Under international Communism the religious and cultural situation will vary almost *toto caelo.* And we must emphasize that Christians in America are not standing in judgment over their European brethren because of some easy or uneasy compromises. The *aliquando conversus* of St. Luke's Gospel was meant for each of us: "And when thou art converted, strengthen thy brethren" (Luke 22:32).

Social Science or Theological Analysis?

A study of the "liturgical" aspects of the ideologies might have been undertaken also by a social scientist. The sociologist would set out from the hypothesis that, through the dynamic interaction of individuals and groups, societies construct their own realms of meaning by creating a variety of symbols—religious and political, educational and legal, artistic and economic. These symbol systems become the means by which society provides the individual with a sense of its acceptable values, of belonging, of permanence in the midst of social change. Symbols are the images of meanings which groups find in or ascribe to the multifarious activities and strata of life.[4] The depth psychologist might find in the ideologies certain patterns of behavior stamped into the collective unconscious of man the hunter during 600,000 years of life spent in the chase. The data is available to the systematic, empirical approach of what is understood as the scientific method. The structure of the ideologies and their sociological manifestations bear a remarkable similarity to the features of Christianity. The social functioning of

[4] Cf. Albert Salomon, "Symbols and Images in the Constitution of Society," *Symbols and Society,* ed. Lyman Bryson (New York: Harper and Brothers, 1955), pp. 103-33.

6

Christianity as an institutional religion in a given country is remarkably similar to the social dynamic of Marxism or of the German Christians. Raymond Aron points to the universality, dogma, and discipline offered by Communism, and he interprets Roman Catholicism and Communism as "rival churches" in France and Italy.[5]

A nuance of this approach is apparent in the argument that Christianity, as a form of social adjustment and control, is useful. In one way or another, all the totalitarian regimes judge religion in terms of its usefulness in the social sphere. But beyond such considerations lies the question whether, in any ultimate sense, Christianity is true; thus the Christian faith must finally present its claim on the solid grounds of its truthfulness. If one's measure for establishing the validity of Christianity or the ideologies were simply their functional utility, their ability to meet human needs, then what accomplishes this purpose most adequately must necessarily be judged the best. However, the writer protests the attempt of many social scientists to give an adequate interpretation of Christianity simply by describing the social ethos and psychological adjustments it engenders.

A comparative study of the rites and symbols of the ideologies cannot set out to establish or "prove" the superiority of Christianity over secular alternatives. All arguments for Christianity on the basis of social effectiveness or adequacy in the face of religious need do not take one beyond social and religious relativism.[6] Though there are structural affinities between Christian doctrines and ideological tenets, and though adherence to these tenets reveals much regarding the religious propensities of man, these factors do not point unambiguously and conclusively to the Christian faith or to any particular Christian denomination. The Christian understanding of history, the rites of Christian worship, and, possibly,

[5] Raymond Aron, *The Century of Total War* (Boston: The Beacon Press, 1955), pp. 139-40.
[6] Cf. Hannah Arendt, "Understanding Communism," *Partisan Review*, XX, 5 (1953), 581-83.

the pattern of Christian social ethics, will seem less quaint after a reading of the documents translated here; but this evidence of affinity provides, in itself, no proof of truth or falsehood. Undeniable evidence of borrowing from the Christian heritage can be adduced, and some evidence for the inadequacy and false optimism of these "spiritual" solutions to human problems may be established. Nevertheless, such evidence does not point exclusively to Christian faith. St. Augustine's insistence on the priority of faith is still relevant: "Unless you believe, you shall not understand." The continued relevance as well as the coherence of the Christian understanding of life as it confronts the symbols of the ideologies constitutes a significant but distinctly limited confirmation of the Christian answer. Certainly the Christian answer is a safeguard against the fatuous hopes of the ideologists, but the truth of Christianity is to be discovered in knowing and doing the truth rather than in demonstrating the hollowness of "substitute religions."

We are constantly reminded today of the tentative nature of scientific and political world-views, and a similar interpretation is given of religion and theologies; the Christian religion and conflicting systems of Christian theology seem particularly vulnerable to this interpretation. There would appear to be nothing unique about Jesus the Messiah, and little effort is needed to show that particular theological formulations are conditioned by their cultural and historical context. The charge of the Enlightenment against religious institutions was their irrational character, and this same charge is raised against the Christian churches by adherents of the ideologies. If the approach to the study of Christianity and the ideologies is simply functional there can be no basis for positing any superiority or prerogative on the part of the Christian faith. In any case, the writer is working in the conviction that the ideologies can only be adequately interpreted from a theological perspective. Within this perspective the actual data of Christianity's unique, historical context must be given more adequate consideration than it usually receives from social scientists. The truth claims of Christianity are inextricably bound up with certain unique historical events. One can and must say this despite what Kierke-gaard rightly says of the "objective uncertainty" of the historical events of Christianity.[7] Whatever Christianity says about man's salvation from sin or his knowledge of God is rooted in the pri-mary actions and purposes of God on the plains of history. Though certain events in the history of a political movement as-sume decisive importance, the truth claims of the ideology are "expressed" in these events rather than "rooted" in them. One must finally choose between the objective, historical framework of the Christian faith and the modern, subjective symbols of the *sym-bolistes* and ideologists.

Moreover, there are dimensions of the ideologies and of Christi-anity, particularly as they involve one's understanding of man, which require different concepts and methods from those of the social sciences. Only a theological framework can properly illumi-nate man's propensities to evil. If one denies the relevance of a theological analysis of the ideologies he will be working with a truncated view of reality. In Kierkegaard's terms, he will be oper-ating on the ethical stage; he will not be directed toward the eter-nal. The implicit rejection of anything ultimate and absolute in man's cultural institutions is, significantly, a part both of the great ideologies and of the method of the social sciences as they have studied these social myths. The great prerogative of the Christian view of life lies in its provision of a decisive center from which to launch a critique of historically contingent values which assume ultimate proportions. One can thereby relate himself, again in Kierkegaard's terms, absolutely to the absolute and relatively to the relative. Faith in a creative source of life which precedes and transcends social, political, and economic institutions serves as a basis for criticism of every partial and particular value.

[7] Cf. *Concluding Unscientific Postscript,* trans. David F. Swenson and Walter Lowrie (Princeton: Princeton University Press, 1941), pp. 25 ff.

2

RELIGION AS IDEOLOGY

JESUS *was a good man. What we need are a lot more people like Him. Now, take Lincoln.* . . .
"AXIOMS FROM AMERICA," *Man's Disorder and God's Design* (1948)

The whole course of Western European history is checkered with the interplay of national-political motives with ecclesiastical loyalties. Already in the ancient Near East rulers made religion an important handmaiden to statesmanship, and the practice is evident everywhere on the American scene today. The observation that in America preachers tend to act like politicians and politicians talk like preachers sums up this point. The most important problem confronting the churches in American public life today lies in the widespread use of the name of Jesus Christ for political purposes. European visitors to our shores in the nineteenth century already observed how central religion and morality were for American politics.[1] Although observers like de Tocqueville and Francis Grund marveled at the separation of church and state attained here they were even more surprised to observe an effect opposite to what they anticipated. Instead of driving religion out of public life it ensconced religion in the manners and mores of the family and of the community and, thereby, laid hold on public opinion. Francis Grund had the perception and the perspective to note ideological features in American piety:

Religion has been the basis of the most important American settlements; religion kept their little community together, religion assisted them in their revolutionary struggle; it was religion to which they appealed in defending their rights, and it was religion, in fine, which

[1] Cf. Jerald C. Brauer, "Images of Religion in America," *Church History,* XXX, 1 (March, 1961), 3-18.

11

taught them to prize their liberties. It is with the solemnities of religion that the Declaration of Independence is yet annually read to the people from the pulpit, or that Americans celebrate the anniversaries of the most important events in their history. It is to religion they have recourse whenever they wish to impress the popular feeling with anything relative to their country; and it is religion which assists them in all their national undertakings. The Americans look upon religion as a promoter of civil and political liberty; and have, therefore, transferred to it a large portion of the affection which they cherish for the institutions of their country.[2]

Religion and morality became necessary for the welfare of American society. They became a social necessity. No candidate for public office was considered trustworthy if he failed to exhibit basic Protestant piety. Religion was the instrument for maintaining a stable society.

In America today the churches are lauded as the bulwark of democracy. Christianity and democracy, together, became our sole defense against Communism. In vast areas of the American scene, Christianity has become a form of culture religion rooted in traditional, social values. This form of Christianity differs little from the comfortable, pietistic Protestantism of Germany before Hitler. There is the same easy identification of religious and social issues—particularly when these are "fundamental" tenets of biblical revelation and "fundamental" principles of free enterprise. There is a new and even more dangerous alliance between religion and personal happiness. In one way or another Christianity becomes a beneficial religion.

The Usefulness of American Piety

The Christian faith, if not quite true, is nevertheless held to be useful in the present crisis. The side effects of a return to Christianity should at least be useful. The utility of religion is seen in the conservative note it gives society. It has long been

[2] Francis Grund, *The Americans in Their Moral, Social, and Political Relations* (London: Longman, Rees, Orme, Brawn, Green & Longman, 1837), I, 294. Quoted by Brauer, *op. cit.*, p. 5.

recognized that a close relationship has prevailed between religious beliefs and convictions and a conservative social program. The Christian religion has been encouraged and promoted as an adjunct to state policy. Necker, the French minister of finance on the eve of the Revolution, brought out the bland cynicism of this attitude when he observed that when taxes are increased it is necessary to increase religious instruction. This view is simply a modulation of Henry IV's conclusion that "Paris is well worth a mass." Generations of the French aristocracy rallied behind a tottering Roman Catholic Church simply because church and aristocracy shared common resentments toward the proletarian masses.

Christian beliefs and ethical principles are frequently invoked by our political orators for their own ends. Franklin D. Roosevelt employed the "God stuff," as he is said to have called it, to soften resistance to his programs. The decade just passed, conveniently denominated "the Eisenhower years," represents the wedding of political sentiment and generalized religion. Eisenhower's campaigns were crusades for moral and spiritual values. Religion endorsed the purposes of America, "the mightiest power which God has yet seen fit to put upon his footstool."[3] The old sacred symbols can be used so effectively because they enjoy broad acceptance by diverse groups in the American populace. The forms are cherished even when the content has been lost. They are understood on many different levels of insight and by citizens who share few other things in common. The sharp words of Rabbi Maurice Eisendrath, president of the Union of American Hebrew Congregations, do not miss the point:

Man is the beginning and end of present-day American religiosity—God is made to serve, or rather to subserve man, to subserve his every purpose and enterprise whether it be economic prosperity, free enterprise, security, or peace of mind. God thus becomes an omnipotent servant, a universal bell-hop, to cater to man's every

[3] Dwight D. Eisenhower, quoted in William Lee Miller, *Piety Along the Potomac: Notes on Politics and Morals in the Fifties* (Boston: Houghton Mifflin, 1964), p. 34.

caprice; faith becomes a sure-fire device to get what we petulantly and peevishly crave. This reduction of God from master to slave has reached its height, or rather its depth of blasphemy, in the cult of the Man Upstairs—the friendly neighbour-god who dwells in the apartment just above. Call on him any time—especially if you are feeling blue. He does not get the least bit upset with your faults and failings and, as for your sins, not only does he not remember them . . . but the very word and concept of sin have been abolished and "adjustment" or "non-adjustment" have taken their places.[4]

Given the passionate desire of Americans for personal security, religion is frequently presented as the ready-made answer to this quest. Religion will protect America against everything, from Communism to "creeping liberalism." The nation can rely on the support, on the moral fiber, which religion provides. It buoys up soldiers and civilians when challenged by Communism's inexorable zeal. It will counteract the temptations to subversion from within. And a new divine sanction is accorded public acts by the acquiescence of the churches.

John Dewey conceded no value to religion except as it expresses the fundamental unities of life. His *Common Faith* bears certain resemblances to the common faith which inspired the German nation under Hitler. Many saw in the entirely new order, the vast social reconstruction undertaken under Franklin Delano Roosevelt, the final realization of Christian beliefs in American social life. Usually the goal envisioned in such "faiths," however, is that devotion be transferred from the Christian faith to some form of the democratic ideal. There have been not a few voices raised to urge that democracy be the real object of devotion in America's churches and synagogues.[5] Public schools, too, should teach the democratic ideal as America's religion; they would be teaching a "community religion" whereas the churches would instill "private

---

[4] Quoted by Cecil Northcott, "America Goes to Church," *The Manchester Guardian Weekly,* September 19, 1957. Used by permission.

[5] Cf. J. Paul Williams, *What Americans Believe and How They Worship* (New York: Harper, 1952), pp. 367-75.

religion."[6] According to J. Paul Williams' proposal, both churches and public schools would be teaching democracy as ultimate metaphysical truth. At present both of them are going about their true task haphazardly and unsystematically. They must concentrate on two elements: *metaphysical sanctions,* i.e., "open indoctrination of the faith that the democratic ideal accords with ultimate reality . . . that democracy is the very Law of Life," and *ceremonial reinforcement,* which would recall and glorify the democratic values, producing a "devotion to democratic ideals like the devotion given by ardent believers in every age to the traditional religions."[7]

Only a minority in the American churches seems to recognize that in such a union Christian faith emerges as a pitiful adjunct to political interest. Christianity is made to bless America's righteous crusade against godless Communism, for God must be on the side of those who persist in invoking him. There is little recognition on the American scene of the very exacting standards of God's righteousness. Christianity is glibly presented as a gospel of personal happiness and success, of peace and well-being. People are unable to bear the biblical warning of judgment and its call to earnest repentance. The prophets of the Old Testament saw divine judgment at the moment of vaunted success and despair in the midst of rejoicing. It was when the land was unable "to bear all his words," when the prophet was asked to "flee away to the land of Judah" (Amos 7:10 ff.), that the disturbing word had to be spoken.

Hitler's View of Christianity

In America, as in Hitler's Germany, the Christian church, as one of the institutions of the nation's culture, is seen as socially useful because of the obedience it fosters. Hitler was willing to leave the churches alone if they would not interfere with temporal affairs. They could concern themselves with matters of another world. They were to confine themselves to the Bible and

[6] *Ibid.,* p. 371.
[7] *Ibid.*

eternal life, leaving this life, men's physical and social well-being, to Hitler. They could be tolerated if they deferred to Nazi ideology as the supreme authority. Bishop Nygren recounts a conversation with a German Nazi jurist in Denmark in 1934. The jurist averred that the Nazi movement would not attack Christianity, but he added, *"nur nichts gegen die nationale Weltanschauung*—only nothing against the nationalist conception of life."[8] Through his 1933 Concordat with the Vatican Hitler gained the dissolution of the Roman Catholic political organization and trade unions. He sought to make Protestantism, too, an instrument of National Socialist politics, a sanction to party politics and activities, through the election of outspoken Nazi sympathizers to church offices. Reference to political measures or the National Socialist *Weltanschauung* in sermons or teaching was declared a criminal offense. The movement even became quite specific on the nature of religion as servant, as may be seen in the following document from the periodical issued for Hitler's elite Black Corps:

> "Today, more than ever, the National Socialist State
> must bear witness, in all its arrangements and organiza-
> tions, to the world-view which has created it and which
> sustains it."

This statement by the Führer, made in his concluding speech at the 1936 Party Congress, amounts to a watchword. Everything said and signified by these words slowly becomes clearer when one looks into the area of practice. I would like now to give all readers a little insight into the way in which the National Socialist State as a state bears witness to its world-view and forms its political life from its world-view.

Surely our religiousness, our faith in our people and its future, stands firmly with both feet on the ground. But let no one come with the objection that such ideas "attempt to find in 'conscience' and its categorical imperative an ersatz for God deposed."

We decline to have our most sacred convictions characterized as pseudo-religion, as though our faith were of less value than that of

[8] Gustav Aulén, *Church, Law, and Society* (New York: Charles Scribner's Sons, 1948), p. 30.

16

the confessional circles. We believe in eternity just as the churchly Christians do. And if we believe that the forces which gave our people the moral impulse for conversion from death-imparting ways are just as "religious" as those hierarchical notions, almost buried under medieval dogmas, which constitute the real kernel of present-day church doctrine, then this is because we are able to see and experience the eternal even in this present world.

A feature which Christianity, wherever it was and is found, has always preserved and cultivated . . . the abstruse doctrine of original sin, which, in fact, first sets the stage for any redemption . . . is intolerable for men of the Nordic race. It cannot be harmonized with the heroic world-view of our blood.

Above all confessional conflicts about matters of opinion—and in Germany today debates regarding religious questions can never be more than this—stands the incontestable fact that for the future of our people everything depends, as a matter of primary importance, on religion as servant of the state creating new spiritual forms designed to help realize the heroic life-ideal of our race. Then, and only then, can the end be achieved that Christianity—which today yet, unfortunately, is predominantly determined by Southern influences—will actually be uprooted among our people. As you know, Germany was unable, for the thousand years following its forced Christianization, to achieve this end.[9]

Spanish and Communist Use of the Churches

Recent experiences have given Christian churches a keener insight into the ease with which they can be used for propaganda purposes. In Spain, for example, Franco has skillfully identified his regime with the Roman Catholic Church. Privileges and prestige are heaped upon the church in recognition of its support of the regime.[10] The church's religious, social, and educational program has encountered few hindrances, but the future may wreak fearful vengeance on a compliant church. Underneath the surface of Spanish life throbs an anti-clericalism which claims huge sections of the Spanish masses, and people spurn the sacraments be-

[9] *Schwarzes Korps,* No. 1 (January 7, 1937). (See Appendix 1 for additional details on some of the Nazi publications cited in the text.)

[10] Cf. Lawrence Fernsworth, *Spain's Struggle for Freedom* (Boston: Beacon Press, 1957), pp. 287-92.

cause of the church's cooperation with Fascism.[11] Key functions of state are never without a mass or without ecclesiastical functionaries: these become necessary features of Franco's "true Christian society." When, in 1943, some doubt existed regarding the allegiance of the bishops, Franco exacted an ironclad oath of allegiance. To be disloyal to the state means what it meant in Czarist Russia, to be disloyal to Christ and his church. Socialism and anticlericalism are equally anathema.[12]

A favorite technique of Communism in dealing with religion has been the establishment of independent "National" or "Progressive" churches. In countries with a Roman Catholic population some wedge has been driven between the body of the faithful, the clergy, the hierarchy, and, finally, Rome. In one way or another the prospect is always offered of more "democratic" control. The actual direction of the new movement, however, has always fallen to a new type of socially progressive, "liberated" pastor or priest. It is possible that the international character of Roman Catholicism can be countered only in this way.

These "reformed" churches, whether Protestant or Roman Catholic, possess a value far beyond the meager number of clergy and laity who promote them. They are centers of propaganda onslaughts on "reactionary" forces, they are instruments of embarrassment and bewilderment for those loyal to the old organization. In Russia, following World War II, the Moscow patriarchate was exploited as a center of appeal to Orthodox Slavs in the occupied countries: the common religious heritage became a point of contact with the Orthodox dispersed throughout the world. Communist authorities simply followed a pattern, developed much earlier by the Czars, of utilizing piety. These "reformed" churches are expected to nourish the patriotic sentiments of their members; they are expected to be in the forefront of opposition to "imperialism"

[11] Salvador de Madariaga, *Spain, A Modern History* (New York: Praeger, 1958), p. 609.
[12] For Franco's efforts to "reeducate" 500,000 Loyalist prisoners see the *March of Time* film, *Inside Fascist Spain*. Cf. also "Spain Shows the Fascist Post-War World," *Life*, April 19, 1943, pp. 25-29.

and "reaction." When they are no longer useful they will inevitably decay along with all religious phenomena.

Such efforts have, however, met with limited success; only a handful of priests has supported these organizations, and an "agreement" or oath of allegiance extracted from the entire body of bishops has often proved more advantageous. In East Germany the few self-styled "progressive Christians" have been able to present no more convincing stand or program than did the churchmen and theologians who supported Hitler in the church struggle of the thirties, and in Poland the "Pax movement" has not attracted much of a following.[13] The significant feature of present-day Communism's stance with respect to the Christian church is not its scattered attempts to "adopt" the church, something about which Nazism was much more determined, but its clothing itself in the traditional forms of the church and offering itself as a counter-church, something the Nazis also did. That such attempts at adoption or usurpation are a recurring feature of the ideologies and, indeed, are almost endemic in them we shall see in succeeding chapters.

[13] The "progressive Christians" behind the Iron Curtain, seeing certain positive features in the new society in which they live, do not wish to be simply negative or neutral with regard to this new world. Because they see their faith in the Gospel as impelling them to work for justice and reform, they determinedly collaborate with the Communists. When they ask the church to bless this new City of Man they also try to point out that they do not want to commit themselves to the ideology, as Hitler's supporters among the *Deutsche Christen* had. Cf. Albert Gervais, "The Church of Silence," *Cross Currents,* VI (1956), 106-08.

3

THE CELEBRATION OF NEW VALUES

> COMPANIONS *the creator seeks, not corpses, not herds and believers. Fellow creators the creator seeks—those who write new values on new tablets.*
> FRIEDRICH NIETZSCHE, *Thus Spake Zarathustra* (1883)

It was in his forceful *City of God Against the Pagans* that St. Augustine, the "Father of a Thousand Years," interpreted the great gods of old Rome as hypostatized expressions of basic Roman values. In a somewhat similar way one might say that the symbols of the ideologies hypostatize the values of the ideology—humanity, scientific objectivity, productive work, patriotism, racial purity, social solidarity. In place of the headings common in Christian theology for centuries one meets new tenets and new values, similar in structure and function to the doctrines they replace, but stemming from a strangely different universe and leading to radically different ends. In this chapter we shall examine some of the new values and their relation to the tenets they have replaced. The ideologies celebrate these values, i.e., they reinforce their centrality through press and radio and through the schools. These new clusters of concern and commitment become basic components of the social myth. The myths form the backdrop for discussion and appear in transfigured form in the symbols and rites which will be considered later.

The Appeal to Science

In one way or another, each of the ideologies invokes the scientific method and lays claim to scientific objectivity. Since the sixteenth century the achievements of physics and mathematics have been so remarkable that the *claim* had at least to be made that the natural sciences were on one's side. In contrast, biblical tenets could be discredited as being mythical and imprecise. The "Hebrew old clothes," in Thomas Carlyle's words, were to be discarded by reasonable men, and strictly conceptual thinking was to be introduced to take their place. Such conceptual thinking was felt to be more accurate and less overlaid with superstition than picture thinking.[1] The new firm ground of social reality was substituted for the spiritual realities of Christianity.

The bases for this development were being laid in the eighteenth and nineteenth centuries. Meanwhile, efforts to find a viable *modus vivendi* between religion and the new science were half-hearted and irresolute. Quite content to know nothing of the wisdom of this world, religion concentrated on the salvation of the individual soul. It castigated the all-embracing scientific aspirations of the medieval scholastics and assumed a role of non-scientific, interior illumination. As the result of its willingness to see nothing more in religion than the relation of the individual soul to God it left Christian people powerless and their claims irrelevant before those of science.

Hannah Arendt points to the connection between scientificality and the rise of the masses. She cites the vision of Enfantin, who could "see the time approaching when the 'art of moving the masses' will be so perfectly developed that the painter, the musician, and the poet will possess the power to please and to move with the same certainty as the mathematician solves a geometrical problem, or the chemist analyses any substance."[2] In the name of scientific socialism, present generations, the middle-aged, and aged, have been sacrificed for the sake of future generations. An action motivated by religious devotion and zeal is undertaken in the name of scientific planning. This is true of Communism, but it was true of Nazism, too. The planning of these regimes rests on no less

[1] Cf. J. V. Langmead Casserley, *The Retreat from Christianity in the Modern World* (New York: Longmans, Green and Co., 1952), pp. 48-51.

[2] *The Origins of Totalitarianism* (London: George Allen and Unwin, Ltd., and New York: Harcourt, Brace and Company, 1951), p. 337. The quotation is from the Saint-Simonist magazine, *Producteur*, I, 339.

than "scientific" certitude. Confidence in science has resulted in the techniques for social planning and control, the pseudo-science of race theory, the forced confessions, the earth satellites, and the techniques of counter espionage. In *The Brothers Karamazov* Ivan represents this trust in man's rational and scientific powers: the world of the future will be shaped on the basis of reason, with no niche left for God.

The German of the twentieth century was told that he must renounce the myths of Asia Minor and turn to a new myth, built on the firmest scientific principles and inhering in his blood. This myth became the central feature of the Nazi ideology. Births, marriages, deaths, and commemorative days in the annual cycle were all tied to the continuity of the people's blood. Selection and preservation of racial and hereditary *(erbgesundheitlich)* "good blood" was "the cardinal point of the future and the source of all divine knowledge."[3] Few people could believe that the Nuremberg Laws on Citizenship and Race could form the basis for a great nation's internal and external policies. The forger of this new myth was Alfred Rosenberg, who developed and propagated Nazi doctrine in his many books and in the Party organs *Völkischer Beobachter* and *NS Monatshefte.* German *Blut und Boden* ("Blood and Soil") were endowed with a mystical splendor; they were unimpeachable in argument and invincible on the field of battle. Fantastic proposals were made and, what is far worse, actually carried out in order to protect "good blood." Rosenberg himself actually executed Nazi racial policies in the occupied territories in the East. The predominance of biological concepts in Nazi ideology—blood, race, Aryan—evidence the absurd lengths to which pseudo-science can be carried in such an "advanced" culture.

This policy, centering on "good blood," shaped German expansion, education, legislation, colonization, morality, eugenics, sterilization, and extermination.[4] The festivals of Nazism, revealed at

---

[3] *Die Feier,* p. 32.

[4] Cf. the racial theory propounded in *The Nazi Primer,* trans. with preface by Harwood L. Childs (New York: Harper, 1938), *passim.*

their clearest in the SS brotherhood, reveal the centrality of blood and kinship. The *Führerprinzip* and the concept of *Lebensraum* were intimately bound to racial theory. The *Deutsche Christen* ascribed a cultic significance to "earth" in the *cultus creatoris,* and "earth" became the bearer, the mother-soil for the mystic "folk." Even the old Nordic institution of blood revenge was reinstated by the Nazis; in connection with the plot of July 20 Himmler assured the leaders of the SS that the family of Graf von Stauffenberg would be "rooted out to the last member of the whole clan."[5] Thus genetics became the determinative science for Nazism, as economic science determines all Communist activities. Through this community of common blood Nazism was able to initiate a unity and solidarity which stood in sharp contrast, so it was held, to French, English, and American disharmony. The Christian heritage from Germany's past was either tolerated, when it promised to confine its teaching to the afterlife, or it was treated as an abject, poisonous, foreign intrusion into the original Nordic spirit and original Nordic purity. In the background the hard core of Nazi ideologists awaited the day when National Socialist science could be pronounced the state religion.

As the race concept formed the core of the Nazi ideology so the class concept determines Communism. In sharp contrast to the Nazi glorification of power, Communist ideology invokes the day when all power will be eliminated in social life. Man's reason will guide him out of the morass of primitive superstition in religion and bourgeois values and will lead him to an enlightened social order, where the old ignorance, exploitation, and suppression will have given way to knowledge, common ownership, and freedom.[6] The assumption is made that an image of the good life can be constructed and that one need only call upon the planners and administrators to achieve one's reasonable, scientific ends. In each

---

[5] "Rede Himmlers über den 20. Juli," *Vierteljahreshefte für Zeitgeschichte,* I, 4 (1953), 385.

[6] Cf. Appendix 2, "Basic Considerations . . . in Stalinstadt."

of the ideologies the cognitive faculty of man has been elevated to a position of preeminence; it so overshadows other faculties that, according to a Christian view of man, one must necessarily misuse man because one does not truly know him.

It is always on the basis of its "scientific materialism" that Communism defends its interpretation of previous history and its triumphant intervention in present history. A. I. Timeniev declares in *Marxism and Modern Thought,* "Only Marxism, only the ideology of the advanced revolutionary class, is scientific."[7] Again and again one meets the ceremonial repetition of the doctrine that only Marxist thought is based on scientific principles; all other thought bears the marks of idealistic or mystical misconceptions, or ideological taint. The world is regarded as intelligible, and war must be waged on whatever is secret or hidden. Joseph C. Bocheński summarizes this feature as follows in his "Formal Structure of Communism":

> The rationalistic mind of modern man is addressed by the "scientific" character of Communism: it sketches a system based on reason and planning, a system in which everything is worked out scientifically and is governed by scientific knowledge. The results of modern science are so amazing and its prestige is so great that this attitude exercises another mighty drawing force on the mind of modern man, but particularly on the intellectual.[8]

The Message of New Life

Both the French *philosophes* and the great German philosophers had used the tools of the age of reason to hammer down the fixed cosmos of medieval philosophy and science. But when they had destroyed men's hopes for a salvation extending through and beyond this life, dynamic new hopes entered to take their place: the expectation of a this-worldly salvation lying somewhere

[7] N. I. Bukharin *et al., Marxism and Modern Thought,* trans. Ralph Fox (New York: Harcourt, Brace, 1935), p. 310.

[8] Bocheński and Gerhart Niemeyer, *Handbuch des Weltkommunismus* (Freiburg-München: Karl Alber, 1958), p. 16.

in the future, proclaimed by the great heralds of better things for this life. These hopes have been affirmed with a passion, a certainty, and a buoyancy which have, traditionally, been associated with the religions of redemption. Rousseau was one of the first to proclaim the message; of his New Gospel Albert Camus says:

> We are witnessing the dawn of a new religion with its martyrs, its ascetics, and its saints. To be able to estimate the influence achieved by this gospel, one must have some idea of the inspired tones of the proclamations of 1789. Fauchet, confronted with the skeletons discovered in the Bastille, exclaims: "The day of revelation is upon us. . . . The very bones have risen at the sound of the voice of French freedom; they bear witness against the centuries of oppression and death, and prophesy the regeneration of human nature and of the life of nations." Then he predicts: "We have reached the heart of time. The tyrants are ready to fall." . . . Scaffolds seemed to be the very altars of religion and injustice. The new faith could not tolerate them. But a moment comes when faith, if it becomes dogmatic, erects its own altars and demands unconditional adoration.[9]

The founding fathers of the United States were steeped in a similar philosophy of the Enlightenment. George Washington and Thomas Jefferson, Benjamin Franklin and James Madison all elevated the democratic attitude toward religious tenets to the rank of the ultimate in religion. They accorded final authority to devotion to freedom of the human spirit, to the powers of reason, to the rights of man and to justice, to human brotherhood on a universal scale. The founding fathers are incessantly eulogized for their religiousness, but few realize the broad expanses of distinctly democratic experience to which they accorded theological status. When, in his early public utterances as president, Dwight D. Eisenhower frequently played upon spiritual themes, he was invoking the same broad creed. There are no marks of the authoritarian personality here and no savior-complex. But there is a strange

[9] *The Rebel: An Essay on Man in Revolt,* trans. Anthony Bower (New York: Vintage Books, 1958), p. 117. Used by permission of Alfred A. Knopf, Inc.

identification of religious belief with democratic values. Martin Marty has arranged some of Eisenhower's basic statements in sequence. A broad democratic creed, the core of the official American faith, emerges:

> I believe in democracy.
> A democracy cannot exist without a religious base.
> Free government is the expression of a deeply felt religious faith.
> You cannot simply explain free government in any other terms than religious.
> This is the faith that teaches us all that we are children of God.
> This faith teaches us that our ideals of democracy and freedom . . . are eternal laws of the human spirit.
> The founding fathers wrote this religious faith into our founding documents . . . they put it squarely at the base of our institutions.
> Happily our people have always reserved their first allegiance to the kingdom of the spirit.
> America is the mightiest power which God has yet seen fit to put upon his footstool.
> America is great because she is good.[10]

However, the theological aspirations of spokesmen for the American dream must be differentiated sharply from totalitarian ventures. In the totalitarian movements the Party is a conspiracy rather than a vehicle of legitimate discussion and pressure in the public forum. Governments have become "proletarianized," in the classical sense, where the elite is in the society but not of it. These governments use against their own people the same methods usually reserved for subject, colonial people.[11] This can be said of the National Socialist Party (the "Nazi" party), the Communist Party in the United States and in various lands, and the John Birch Society. Totalitarianism consistently demonstrates its hostility to every voluntary organization of an occupational or religious nature. Al-

[10] Martin E. Marty, *The New Shape of American Religion* (New York: Harper, 1959), p. 83. Used by permission of the publisher.
[11] Cf. the article by Franklin H. Littell on "Totalitarianism" in Littell and Hans Hermann Walz (eds.), *Weltkirchenlexikon: Handbuch der Oekumene* (Stuttgart: Kreuz-Verlag, 1960), cols. 1466-69.

though one can trace tendencies in the direction of totalitarianism on American ground, one still faces the fortunate lack of full flower.

It was faith in another dynamic new message that Nazi ideologists instilled into the German *Wehrmacht.* Yet for Himmler this vision was insufficient. Speaking of the Wehrmacht, which he identified *in toto* with the plot on Hitler, he said, "The faith in a renewal on a vast scale was not apparent in this army."[12]

The bearer of this message in Nazism was the myth of a new chosen people. In ironic similarity to the hated Jewish "swine," this people was the new "holy nation" which must oppose materialistic ideals and interests. The Nazis had been "elected" by God to achieve their unique historic destiny, and they were prepared to face the corresponding rejection and destruction if they should prove unfaithful. Nevertheless, as Hannah Arendt has pointed out, Nazism did not confine its interests to the national state. The anti-Semitic central core forced it to a supranational approach to politics. As in the case of Communism, "the movement" was more important to the Nazis than territorial boundaries.[13]

But there is also the concept of Holy Russia. The Russian people have for centuries been guided by the myth of a messianic destiny. They have seen themselves as a people set apart from others. In the words of Shatov in Dostoevsky's *Devils,* Russia was a "god-bearing nation." Though God is infinite and universal, the Father of all men, yet he must stand in a unique relationship to Russia, the only holy land. As the children of Israel were a living witness to the God of the Old Covenant so the Russian people were a witness to another god. After the apostasies of "Old Rome" and "New Rome" God had finally transferred the divine throne of

[12] "Rede Himmlers über den 20. Juli," *op. cit.*
[13] Hannah Arendt, *The Origins of Totalitarianism.*

his apostolic church to "the third Rome." Starets Filofey of Pskov (d. 1547) gives concise expression to this unique status:

> . . . for know, thou devout one, that all Christian realms have run their course and all together have passed over into the realm of our ruler, in keeping with the prophetic books. Such is the Russian Empire. For two empires have fallen, but the third stands, and there will be no fourth.[14]

Still Russian Communism, though it is capable of assigning a distinctive place to the national mission, has never ceased to proclaim a message of universal salvation. When Russia was renewed and regenerated it would purify and rejuvenate the West. A vision of harmonious working of all classes of society, of economic plenty, of technical efficiency, of cultural and athletic invincibility now animates the Soviet man. Men are assured that they can and are saving themselves because the first fruits of the new life are already present among them.

The Interpretation of Man

In each of the ideologies we meet a lofty conception of man, both as he truly is in the present and as he promises to be in the future. Crèvecoeur saw such a conception in the democratic ideology which pervaded the American frontier. He is fascinated by the American, "a new man, who acts upon new principles."[15] The freedom and limitless spaces spurred, according to Crèvecoeur, the development of a new breed: "Everything has tended to regenerate them; new laws, a new mode of living, a new social system; here they are become men. . . . Here individuals of all nations are melted into a new race of men, whose labours and posterity will one day cause great changes in the world."[16]

---

[14] Quoted by Ernst Benz, *The Eastern Orthodox Church,* trans. Richard and Clara Winston (New York: Anchor Books, 1963), p. 182. Copyright © 1963 by Doubleday and Company, Inc.; reprinted by permission of the publisher.

[15] J. Hector St. John Crèvecoeur, *Letters from an American Farmer,* ed. Warren Barton Blake (New York: E. P. Dutton & Co., 1912), p. 44.

[16] *Ibid.,* pp. 42, 43.

In each of the ideologies the basic optimism of the Enlighten-ment regarding man's nature and possibilities becomes evident. Fol-lowing the lead of Jean-Jacques Rousseau, it is man's social cir-cumstances which are responsible for evil, not his nature, which is inherently "good." Rousseau's reading of man's nature is as basic for democracy's projection of the perfect society as it is for Marx-ism's mission of realizing the classless society. Although the paths to their goal diverge sharply, for both Marx and Rousseau a moral, happy people can be created by rooting out the evils inherent in men's social institutions. By way of contrast, the Christian reading of man's nature seems bleak indeed. One always encounters the assertion that there is a source and root of evil in the individual, that institutional evils are always rooted in personal sin. And the contradictions battling in man's own nature are not overcome in human history but await resolution in the *eschaton,* the fulfillment of the kingdom of God. Expressed more simply, the Christian faith declares that man's relation to God is disturbed in a far more radi-cal manner than the great political myths suppose.

There are, to be sure, vital differences in the understanding of man from ideology to ideology. The romantic and voluntaristic framework of Nazism and Fascism stands poles apart from the reasonable being of the Democratic and Communist world. Fasc-ism and Nazism did not hold that all men were capable of rul-ing: the weak and cowardly could not be counted as capable of governing themselves. Each had its categories of slave people and lordly people. For the Nazis the forces of darkness embraced the Marxists, Free Masons, Jews, Jesuits, "the international plutocracy," and finally even the German General Staff.

Communist theory proposes to renew human society and the in-dividual's life conduct from their very sources. Nothing less than a new order of societal and personal life is satisfactory as a goal. In place of the biblical picture of man created in the image of God there is the Marxist slogan, "We form men according to our image." Man is molded according to the image of the ideal Com-munist citizen. The text for the East German *Jugendweihe* ("Youth

30

Dedication") reveals quite clearly the importance of knowing, trusting in, and of utilizing one's own creative energies. There is no sympathy here for Luther's ringing, "With might of ours can nought be done." As a result the conflict must be seen as finally between faith in man as creator—and Christian theology has often not evaluated the creative capacities of man positively enough—and faith in the creative power of God. In Communism the conviction always emerges that dependence on supernatural powers has vitiated the efforts and initiative of men, thus keeping them from employing all their own energies, consciously and free from all prejudices, for the building of Socialism. Socialist "realism" attempts to celebrate the transformed Socialist man on stage and screen, in literature and painting. This man is concerned only with problems of his present existence, with quotas and seven-year-plans, with humanistic values and social objectives. The heroes of the working class and the people are set in the sharpest contrast with stereotypes of Fascism, imperialism, and militarism.[17] Hannah Arendt discerns in the doctrine of the transformation of human nature the distinguishing mark of the totalitarian phenomenon: "What totalitarian ideologies therefore aim at is not the transformation of the outside world or the revolutionary transmutation of society, but the transformation of human nature itself. The concentration camps are the laboratories where changes in human nature are tested . . . ."[18] The concentration camps have succeeded in refashioning men's minds in a way which hardly falls short of scientific precision.

The history of the ideologies in the modern world reveals that the self cannot long serve as its own end. Men seek an ideal or a faith which will release them from the confinement of self-realization or self-expression. An autonomous loyalty is usually a transitional stage to some form of heteronomy—the party, the cause, or the nation. Reinhold Niebuhr has pointed out in *The Self and the*

[17] Cf. "Der neue sozialistische Mensch," *Kulturspiegel der Sowjetzone,* No. 4 (February 16, 1960).
[18] Hannah Arendt, *The Origins of Totalitarianism,* p. 432.

Dramas of History that the self becomes a self only as it is drawn out of itself by a power which can elicit devotion, but which does not overwhelm the true freedom of the self. This is true of biblical faith, where one casts oneself on the grace and power of God, yet is unable to make these subserve human ends.[19] It is finally only through the dialogue of the self with God that man and the events of history gain a coherent and consistent meaning.

The New Morality

It is the idyll of untainted and uncorrupted human nature that still reigns in the parties descended from Marxism. Selfishness, covetousness, internecine quarrelsomeness, and false values must eventually and inevitably give way to brotherliness, common creativeness, and social solidarity. But meanwhile one must fight the good fight for a just and honest cause; one must be watchful, must steel himself, and must be ready to offer himself in the struggle against the decadent forces of Western imperialism and capitalism. Egoistic motives must give way to the Socialist community of comrades.[20]

So close and so valuable is this comradeship that the Socialist man will always be alert. He will be ready to use arms to defend the brotherhood. A poem by Heinz Czechowski entitled "The New Age" indicates the new virtues:

> The New Age
> Requires a new morality:
> We work, plan, co-rule—
> Rulers without number.
>
> We build industrial combinations,
> Improve an improved world.

[19] *The Self and the Dramas of History* (New York: Charles Scribner's Sons, 1955). Cf. the chapter on "The Self and its Search for Ultimate Meaning" (pp. 61-72) and pp. 255 ff.

[20] Cf. "Auszug aus dem *'Entwurf des Hochschulprogramms der FDJ,'* " *Forum,* April 1, 1957. Reprinted in *Zur Situation der Studenten in der Sowjetzone* (Bonn: Bundesministerium für gesamtdeutsche Fragen, 1957), pp. 40-44.

> We ask for peace
> That what we build may abide.
>
> As long as on the other side
> No friendly state exists,
> We learn the building of a wall,
> But how to shoot as well[21]

The shape of the future explains what is right in the present. Freedom of the workers from the least vestige of exploitation demands the repudiation of traditional moral standards. P. F. Kolonizki writes in his vigorous attack on Christian faith and morals: "The entire ideology of Communism and, along with it, Communist morality, is subordinate to the freeing of the workers. The goal of the Communist is the erection of Communism, to create the highest happiness of the workers, not in legends, but in building through actual deeds a truly paradisaical life here on earth."[22] The attack on Christian morals became quite clear at the fifth Party Congress of the SED (Socialist Unity Party of [East] Germany) in Berlin on July 10, 1958. There Walter Ulbricht announced the "Ten Commandments of Socialist Morality":

> The moral face of the new, Socialist man disclosed in this noble struggle for the victory of Socialism is determined by the observance of the basic moral law:
>
> 1. Thou shalt ever take thy stand for the international solidarity of the working class and of all workers, as well as for the indissoluble alliance of all Socialist countries.
>
> 2. Thou shalt love thy fatherland and be ever ready to devote all thy energy and ability to the defense of the workers' and farmers' power.
>
> 3. Thou shalt aid in the removal of the exploitation of men by men.

---

[21] From *Pressespiegel der Sowjetzone,* No. 16 (April 24, 1962), p. 3.
[22] *Kommunistische und religiöse Moral* (Berlin: Verlag Junge Welt, 1953), p. 20. Reproduced in *Ein Dokument antireligiöser Propaganda aus der Sowjetunion* (Bonn: Bundesministerium für gesamtdeutsche Fragen, 1957). Cf. also Emil Wiederkehr, *Jugend im Bannkreis der roten Moral* (Berne: Hilfskomitee für die Opfer des Kommunismus, 1958), *passim.*

4. Thou shalt do good deeds for Socialism, for Socialism leads to a better life for all workers.

5. Thou shalt build up Socialism in the spirit of mutual help and comradely cooperation, honor the collective, and take to heart its criticism.

6. Thou shalt guard and increase the peoples' property.

7. Thou shalt ever strive for the increase of thine output, be frugal, and establish Socialist workers' discipline.

8. Thou shalt educate thy children in the spirit of peace and of Socialism, to become broadly cultured men, sound in character as well as physique.

9. Thou shalt live a clean and decent life and honor thy family.

10. Thou shalt practice solidarity with those struggling for their national freedom and with those defending their national independence.[23]

It should be noted that, contradictory though the goals of the Kingdom of Man are with those of the Kingdom of God, strong elements of traditional Christian morality are prominent in this decalogue. The virtues of social responsibility, productive work, family unity, and devotion to nation are all here. These are the very elements which a Christianity in retreat from the world long ignored. Ulbricht's Ten Commandments indicate the durability of Christian ethics rather than their demise. Although the Communists have announced a break with Christian morals, they have adapted Christian norms to the erection of Communism. In the official party cultural organs one notes the echo of early Christian opposition to what was false and obsolete in the church's tradition, particularly in its individual and social ethics. But here the complaint is caustic and proud, for the party has pulled old heavens down to earth. In some instances the solid virtues of early Calvinism come to the fore, as in the call of the Chinese Communists to help workers "recognize that they must, under the leadership of the Communist Party, constantly raise their own social consciousness . . . develop the excellent tradition of working hard,

---

[23] Reprinted in *Kirchliches Jahrbuch* (1958), pp. 175-76.

maintain the noble character of being just and selfless, work hard in production, save, and economize."[24]

If one compares "The Ten Commandments of National Socialism" given below with Ulbricht's Ten Commandments he finds some of the same virtues: discipline, comradeship, hard work, unselfishness. But there are also the distinctive Nazi virtues of devotion to the Führer, pride, loyalty, and bravery.[25] Here one sees an explicit statement of the principle that "That is right which serves the movement":

The Führer is always right!
Never violate discipline!
Never waste time in idle talk or in self-gratifying criticism—instead, take hold and create!
Be proud but not arrogant!
The program is your dogma; it demands your complete devotion to the movement!
You are representative of the Party; order your behavior and appearance accordingly!
Loyalty and unselfishness are your supreme commandments!
Evidence real comradeship, and you will be a true socialist!
Do unto your German comrades as you would have them do unto you!
In battle be tough and discreet!
Courage is not foolhardiness!
That is right which serves the movement, and through it Germany, that is, your people![26]

Kingdom of Man against Kingdom of God

The Christian faith asserts that in a fallen world social, economic, and political life will always fall short of the optimistic goals the ideologies set for themselves. In contrast to the infinite and transcendent judgment of history by Jesus Christ as proclaimed

[24] Harriet C. Mills, "Thought Reform: Ideological Remolding in China," *The Atlantic Monthly,* June, 1959, pp. 75-76.

[25] Cf. Appendix 3, "Example of a Worship Service of the German Christians."

[26] From *Organisationsbuch der NSDAP,* ed. Robert Ley (Munich: Franz Eher, 1938), p. 8.

by Christianity the goal one meets in the ideologies is finite and temporal: a final synthesis is expected within history. There is progress in history toward the Kingdom of Man. In the coming millenium of peace, in a state of humanity in which class warfare will have disappeared, man will be able to attain to self-fulfillment. All his legitimate desires will be supplied. A utopian eschatology characterizes both Nazi and Communist thought: in each a form of salvation is offered, in each the beginning of a new cycle of history is announced. A message of salvation is proclaimed within this world, this present age, and man's well-being in this age becomes the measure of all things. This object of faith shapes his life.

Some democratic thinkers, too, have elevated the American experiment into a religious faith. This faith helped America achieve the unity and purpose and destiny which guided her through testing. It was not only the poets, the romanticists, who expressed this faith. But it was Walt Whitman who expressed the hope for the final synthesis of the American "peaceable kingdom" more passionately than others:

> But it is not yet . . . the fully-receiv'd, the fervid, the absolute faith.
>
> I submit, therefore, that the fruition of democracy, on aught like a grand scale, resides altogether in the future. It too [the democratic principle] must be adorned, credited with its results—then, when it, with imperial power, through amplest time, has dominated mankind—has been the source and test of all the moral, esthetic, social, political, and religious expressions and institutes of the civilized world—has begotten them in spirit and in form, and has carried them to its own unprecedented heights—has had (it is possible) monastics and ascetics, more numerous, more devout than the monks and priests of all previous creeds—has sway'd the ages with a breadth and rectitude tallying Nature's own—has fashion'd, systematized, and triumphantly finish'd and carried out, in its own interest, and with unparallel'd success, a new earth and a new man.[27]

---

[27] "Democratic Vistas," from *The Poetry and Prose of Walt Whitman*, ed. Louis Untermeyer (New York: Simon and Schuster, 1949), pp. 830-31. Copyright 1949, Simon and Schuster; reprinted by permission of the publisher.

Walt Whitman admitted that he was a sojourner to a far country but he was happy to be thrust about in the "brave turmoil" and "heart-wearying postponements" of his day if only he might have the hope of the glory which would be revealed.

Whitman's anguish and doubt were stimulated by the throes of the great Civil War. From his desk and on the streets of Washington he had watched Lincoln's agony. Lincoln saw the providential working of God in the history of an "almost chosen people."[28] For Lincoln, God's calling and favor were an indescribably grievous burden, a divine summons to self-sacrifice. It was a call to action under the eyes of a righteous God. It was far removed from Whitman's religious vision of a political church.

According to all of these views it is toward the City of Man that history moves, rather than toward the City of God. The eschatology of National Socialism rested directly on a corrupted biblical and millennial basis. The millennium it proclaimed had, in contrast to the Communist view, already been ushered in. It was beset by demonic forces, but it would prevail by the blessing of destiny. In the Marxist picture the transformation must be preceded by a violent eruption of the proletariat, an event which will pave the way for the redistribution of economic resources. The transformation of man's class-bound social situation is achieved only by dint of Promethean effort, but the final end looms bright and attractive. It is to be well worth the sacrifices of the Revolution, and—in the reinterpretation—the transitional period of Socialist society. Helmut Gollwitzer observes that the Communist reasons: "Marxism must be true, because God does not exist. Because there is no God, Marxism is the only solace. If Marxism were not true, where should we be, since there is no God?" Therefore, says Gollwitzer, the Communist has "an amazing ability to live in the future and to ignore the present."[29]

---

[28] Cf. William J. Wolf, *The Almost Chosen People: A Study of the Religion of Abraham Lincoln* (New York: Doubleday, 1959); now reissued as *The Religion of Abraham Lincoln* (New York: Seabury, 1963), *passim.*

[29] *Unwilling Journey,* trans. E. M. Delacour (Philadelphia: Muhlenberg Press, 1954), p. 141.

To be sure, Marxists have a great many who sympathize with their faith in the Kingdom of Man. For many democratic thinkers the idea of progress through man's free exercise of his reason has replaced the expectation of an *eschaton;* the historical process is sufficient quite of itself without the requirement for a supernatural consummation. But the conscious opposition to a kingdom not of this world is not present. Engels declared that since the Kingdom of God proclaimed by Christ had not been realized after eighteen hundred years men are justified in turning to a firmer, earthier hope. Engels himself points to the similarities between Socialism and early Christianity: "Both Christianity and the workers' socialism preach forthcoming salvation from bondage and misery; Christianity places this salvation in a life beyond, after death, in heaven; socialism places it in this world, in a transformation of society."[30] It was one of the failures of Christian people that they had so little awareness of the present reality of Christian salvation that the Communist hope seemed the only tangible possibility.

Moreover, participation in these new kingdoms offered a sharing, a fellowship, and a present realization which was lacking in the churches. To be sure, the churches still carried on a ministry in these societies, but the remnant was no longer a "saving remnant," aware of its priestly function in the world. The Fascist and Communist movements, the "political churches," came to the outcasts, "the prodigals and sinners" of society, and pressed them into a kind of priestly work for others. So Peron found his support, from 1946 to 1955, mostly among the workers, the *descamisados,* or "shirtless ones." Hitler gave the Germans meaningful labor, and Lenin offered the people entry into a true workers' and peasants' community.

The Understanding of History

The regime which controls the present controls the past as well.

---

[30] Friedrich Engels, "On the History of Early Christianity," in Karl Marx and Friedrich Engels, *Basic Writings on Politics and Philosophy,* ed. Lewis S. Feuer (Garden City: Doubleday Anchor Books, 1959), p. 168. Copyright © 1959 by Lewis S. Feuer; quotations from this volume are reprinted by permission of Doubleday and Company, Inc.

It controls the writing of history, the interpretation of its own origins and motives. Ancient cities and empires interpreted and justified their past by means of heroic legends. They were able to correct disturbing facts and uncomfortable realities. They ennobled the great men who founded their cities and traditions. When one compares identical events in the historiography of different nations he may see how present interests continue to determine the form of old antagonisms.

The great Renaissance patrons of the arts were already fully aware of the uses of history, but extremes have been reached in the collectivist dictatorships. Successive editions of the "Great Soviet Encyclopedia" have controlled the past for the Russian people, much in the manner depicted by George Orwell in *1984.* In Orwell's prediction we see Winston Smith patiently rewriting party history in the Ministry of Truth. The past is brought up to date; a massive cadre of workers rewrites old numbers of the *Times* and creates new facts and persons, while another section collects and destroys all old documents. Voltaire's quip, "History is after all only a pack of tricks we play on the dead," has never been more accurate than with reference to the historiography found here. Carl Becker has commented, "To him it was a witticism intended to brand dishonest historians, whereas we perceive that it formulated, in the neatest possible way, a profound truth—the truth that all historical writing, even the most honest, is unconsciously subjective, since every age is bound, in spite of itself, to make the dead perform whatever tricks it finds necessary for its own peace of mind."[31] In a Soviet painting depicting Lenin speaking in the Ukraine in 1920 both Trotsky and Kamenev could be conveniently left out.[32] Beria, following his liquidation, is no longer mentioned or referred to in any way. They have become, in Orwell's phrase later popularized by Bertram Wolfe, "unpersons."

[31] *The Heavenly City of the Eighteenth-Century Philosophers* (New Haven: Yale University Press, 1932), p. 44.
[32] *Since Stalin: A Photo History of Our Time* (New York: Swen Publications, 1951), p. 43.

Sketches of party history, each written with personal interests to defend, have come from Lenin, Zinoviev, Trotsky, and Stalin. The versions of Stalin's *Short History of the Communist Party of the Soviet Union* remained incontestable until his death; here Trotsky was denigrated and Stalin was lionized. "Then," as Bertram Wolfe writes, "some 50,000,000 copies were pulped or burned, and the party remained history-less until Khrushchev had sufficiently stabilized his regime and his version of the past to rewrite it once more."[33] The new *History* minimizes the role of Comrade Stalin and elevates the role of the party. Leonard Shapiro says of this "latest venture in imaginative historiography":

> Its purpose rather is to draw a veil over the disagreeable realities of the past and to look to the future; at the same time, it attempts to provide a coherent story, based on "evidence" supposed to be accepted at face value, of the ineluctable, historically predetermined rise of the party. It is a success story, of which "the party" is the hero—always right, always at hand to correct the mistakes of individuals, always the only interpreter of the true path to progress.[34]

Each of the ideologies takes time seriously: time is no illusion and history is made up of no great, recurring cycles. Time is the arena in which man achieves his redemption, by dint of heroic action. There is an inevitable movement of history in the Marxist dialectic; this movement is interpreted as progressive, without reversals and setbacks. In one way or another history is on the side of each of the great movements. For Karl Marx the inevitable dialectic of history moves through four stages of prehistory—the Asiatic, the ancient, the feudal, the bourgeois—to the proletarian epoch. In all of this it is strictly social and economic factors that actually determine the course of events.

[33] Bertram Wolfe, "A Party of a New Type," *Problems of Communism,* IX, 4 (July-August, 1960), 43. In Wolfe's exposition of the Khrushchev version he explores the "disappearance of events." Cf. Wolfe's "New Gospel according to Khrushchev," *Foreign Affairs,* XXXVIII (July, 1960), 576-87.

[34] Leonhard Shapiro, "A New History—A New Mythology," *Problems of Communism,* IX, 1 (January-February, 1960), 60. Reprinted by permission from *Problems of Communism,* Washington, D. C.

In contrast to the Christian hope in the coming of the Kingdom of God at the end of time—the triumphant victory of God over evil principalities and powers—one meets in Communism the expectation of the rule of the proletariat, that ultimate outcome of history when foreign and domestic enemies will have been put under foot and no government will be needed to combat the greed, exploitation, and tyranny of the old bourgeois society. Men can realize the fulfillment of life within a history which is itself "redemptive" because of the progressive elimination of evil, regressive forces. The "harmonious commonwealth," the "classless society," or the "New Order" may be compared with the golden age of ancient legends or with the paradise of Genesis. A new era of fellowship and harmony of all workers and farmers looms on the horizon. History here assumes a character comparable to biblical sacred history: in place of the progressive realization of God's purposes through the enlistment of men in a fellowship of divine service and service to the neighbor, the goal here is a planned society, joint ownership of property, and improved conditions of life for the masses.

For Hitler the course of German history moved through early Germanic greatness, the "stab in the back" during World War I, defeat, reparations, and debasement, on to awakening and the indomitable hegemony of the Third Reich.

Each of the ideologies possesses a broad pattern for history which is designed to lead to understanding and action. Though overly optimistic and doctrinaire, this pattern enables militants to grapple realistically with concrete situations, to promote social planning on a vast scale, to work toward the removal of the tensions and conflicts which characterize life in history. Vast engineering projects and technical efficiency are at the heart of the Soviet endeavor. Science and mathematics become the forms of higher education; heavy industry, hydroelectric stations, atomic energy plants, mechanized agriculture, technical institutes become the backbone of the Marxist experiment. The Communists' conception of progress in history by means of technological advances has made it possible for them to act and to alter the course of history. Their opponents, on the other hand, can be faulted for choosing to retard the march of history: the course of events must inevitably override and destroy reactionary individuals.

If man's only paradise must be located on this earth it is the aim of Communism to inaugurate this paradise in the shortest time possible. Accordingly the cult of a new Jerusalem has been pursued in Communist countries: present enjoyments and even present life-cycles have had to be sacrificed for the future munificence of human welfare. Present generations can only dream of the shape and conditions of life which the future will bring. Children, however, will realize and experience the Communist order of society, when war will have become a phenomenon of the past and the perfect Communist democracy will have been realized. The Chinese comrades confounded and provoked Moscow by claiming that China had already entered the era of Communism. China signalized its material achievement by the slogans "Twenty Years Compressed into One Day" and the "Great Leap Forward."

The philosophers and prime movers of the French Revolution, too, were in common agreement on the tenet that the human condition could be advanced indefinitely by altering the social organism. Public education, the deliberations of reasonable men, new and equitable laws—these were all part of the improvement of society. For the American revolutionaries, too, there was a common conviction that in 1776 a "new order of the ages" (*novus ordo seclorum*) was coming into being. As immortalized on the Great Seal of the United States, the eye of heaven was "favorable to the undertaking" (*annuit coeptis*). These are the words Vergil applies to "pious Aeneas," who enjoyed the favor of the gods in founding the "walls of lofty Rome." Aeneas' was a religious enterprise, and the founding of the American republic was considered no less religious.

Nor can we say that this religious fervor applied to the "holy experiment" was confined to its early years. By its insertion of the words "under God" in the Pledge of Allegiance the United States Congress was pointing to a high, if not unique, degree of divine favor. And by making the familiar affirmation "In God We Trust" the official motto of the United States our Congress was making what logicians call a universal proposition which is patently false.[35] William Lee Miller has observed with respect to this phenomenon: "All religious affirmations are in danger of standing in contradiction to the life that is lived under them, but none more so than these general, inoffensive, and externalized ones which are put together for public purposes."[36] Corporate America's trust in God is at least as attenuated as the Israelites' trust in Jahweh during forty years' wandering. We have an idealized, exalted picture of America as a religious nation, a chosen people, selected and blessed by providence for a peculiar purpose. The early Puritans had some justification for such a claim, but contemporary America—at least during the religious revival of the past decade—has put its faith in faith itself.

The trends in the direction of an American culture religion have been checked by prophetic preaching. But they have been checked as much by the requirement laid upon the American churches to define their message in their mission outreach. So long as a specific and well-articulated system of doctrine and practice was required for evangelistic purposes the threat of a platitudinous religiosity was less real. But when the drive to evangelize declined, both in domestic and foreign missions, the secular religions could bid for a respectable place in the churches. The deterioration of true mission conviction was accompanied by a deterioration in the exercise of church discipline. No definable standards of church membership prevail in vast sections of American Christianity. It is no surprise that new devotions should emerge to take up the slack of lost integrity.

[35] Cf. Sydney E. Ahlstrom, "The Pieties of Usefulness," *Stetson University Bulletin,* LVII, 3 (July, 1957).
[36] William Lee Miller, *Piety Along the Potomac: Notes on Politics and Morals in the Fifties,* p. 46.

Confessional Schools of the Ideologies

At a recent district conference of the Communist Party in Frankfurt on the Oder the huge slogan facing the delegates read: "The Building of Socialism is Primarily a Matter of Educating Men."[37] No task is taken more seriously by the ideologies than is education. The separation of the church from the schools, the exclusion of Christian influences from the public school system, has increasingly become the pattern in European countries. Nineteenth-century nationalism in many European lands had as one of its aims the increased influence of secular and national interests in the nation's schools. In Germany, Hegelian philosophy provided a major impulse in the direction of secular schools; in Italy the educational reform followed the pattern of Gentile's reconstruction; in America John Dewey's educational theory has exercised the strongest influence in the nation's schools.

Communist and Nazi indoctrination both required that the traditional pattern of providing religious instruction in the schools must cease. By capturing the minds of children in the schools these regimes have made their bid to shape the form of the future. Actual tactics have varied, but two features have been prominent: either insuperable difficulties have been placed in the way of Christian instruction, or schools have been forcibly set apart from the church. The following confidential report from Nazi youth headquarters gives a glimpse of the view the Nazis took of instructing the masses:

> . . . *One never fights against something negative, but for something positive!*
> In gaining one's positive goal one smashes the negative to pieces! So the cardinal point of our battle must never be lost in conflict with the negative Catholic Youth. We must press, rather, toward the realization of our goals (Socialism, the program, the elimination of the system of privileges)! Then the *good* will fight with us, and we shall simply give up all claim to the corrupt.

[37] Cf. *Neuer Tag,* June 17, 1960. Reprinted in *Hinter dem Eisernen Vorhang,* No. 25 (Berlin, July 30, 1960), p. 8.

Finally, however, it should not be forgotten that something is to be learned from the systematic method of the Catholic Church which has been tested now for two thousand years. One always strikes each opponent best with his own weapons!

At the outset our Führer had to adopt the highly intuitive and diplomatic methods which are characteristic of the Jesuits. Naturally only the upper echelons [of the Jesuits] employ such methods, and it seems that even today the greater part of the Catholic clergy have been placed in their positions through their influence.

The question emerges whether two different systems of schools should not be set up, one for leaders and the other for followers. Whereas the leaders must receive a highly political, psychological, and comprehensive education, National Socialism must be implanted in the masses doctrinally and dogmatically, in the most primitive manner.

For this reason it is necessary that our training of the masses utilize, at least occasionally, cultic-religious forms. A definite rite for opening and closing an evening at the retreat, with remembrance of the dead (the martyrs) of the Movement, the millions of compatriots in foreign lands, a regular reading from *Mein Kampf* as the Bible of the Movement and from the program as our New Testament (or our Ten Commandments) in conjunction with the singing of our newly composed songs, the "Heil" to the Führer, perhaps also marching in and out with a number of banners—and all of this *regularly* and always in the same form, but with different content— is necessary.

Already in the meetings during the period of struggle the Movement developed the beginnings of such a rite with the opening, the bearing of the banners, the three-fold "Heil," and the "Horst Wessel Song." Would it not be correct to continue in this direction? The Service of the churches, too, is always in the same form; only the theme changes. One cannot say it was simply this rigid form that brought about the demise of the church.

1. Enter a Catholic Church sometime. Eighty per cent of the worshipers are *under* 25 years of age, and of this eighty per cent, two-thirds are men. So the worshipers are by no means old women!

2. Even should the church die out, this would be in no way a result of its forms, which have stood the test of two thousand years, but of the content, which is now outmoded. It is not the rite that alienates people from the church, but, quite the contrary, the churches are indebted to the rite for existing any more at all. No,

45

the stuff treated there no longer interests people; it has been proven untrue and a fabrication of lies; it has been overtaken by science, and so has been discarded by the people. But how stable a system would be if it were to apply the same psychologically sound and successful methods to the most accurate, the most modern, and the most scientific world-view.

3. For the broad masses, dogmas and forms, something to which even the simplest man can cling, are simply necessary. It is not merely a matter of having the use of these dogmas and forms harden into law through centuries-old usage, so that one can take one set of dogmas away only by giving people others. It is rather the case of a particular group's being able to understand only the superficial aspects of any world-view, even the simplest. For this reason the content must be made available to them in the briefest, most under-standable, and most primitive formulas.[38]

In the effort to achieve ideological uniformity it has often been found insufficient to separate the school from the church. The logic of this pattern points to a single school system, with no pa-rochial or private schools, i.e., a state monopoly in the field of education. Peron, for example, finally felt he required the full and unqualified support which complete control of the school system would give him, and it was because of opposition on this issue that he was overthrown. For each of the totalitarian systems edu-cation of children has ceased to be a private matter and has be-come a responsibility of society. Home and church are excluded from the educational process in East Germany today by a terse law: "The academic education and formation of the young is the exclusive concern of the state."[39]

All influences militating against ideological uniformity must be dissolved: the minds of the *total* population must be brought into conformity with the ideology. As Bishop Dibelius has pointed out with reference to the Nazis, Communists, and even the Social Democrats, under the claim of wishing to "de-confessionalize" the

[38] *Informationsdienst,* October 28, 1935.

[39] "Gesetz über die sozialistische Entwicklung des Schulwesens in der Deutschen Demokratischen Republik," December 2, 1959. Reprinted in *Die katholische Kirche in Berlin und Mitteldeutschland* (Berlin: Morus-Verlag, 1962), p. 30.

schools these groups have really wanted to replace Christian faith with their political creed.[40] The state schools developed into confessional schools of the racial or materialist world-view.

The pattern in one country after another behind the Iron Curtain has been the nationalization of church schools: buildings, equipment, and funds have become state property, and neither funds nor materials are permitted for the construction or maintenance of private schools. Teachers are employed by the state and a completely secular, if not atheistic, trend is evident in classroom instruction. To be sure, the traditional Catholicism of Poland has forced a notable exception; but the agreement is uneasy, and no one doubts the party's intentions. When children are required, as part of their homework, to write short essays parroting their Communist instruction, and when parents are expected to read and sign their children's essays, the effect can only be demoralizing for pupil, teacher, and parents, none of whom can accept the words of the other as true. And if, as in Estonia, religious education must be confined to confirmation instruction during the summer months, the educational task of the church is severely restricted. During the school year the Christian ethos is inundated by an alien faith.

In East Germany the so-called Lange Decree was designed to drive a wedge between young people and confirmation instruction. The decree requires that an interval of at least two hours elapse between the close of school and any extra-curricular instruction. The reason given is that the child should have time to recover his "physical and mental powers." The following are excerpts from the "Ordinance to Assure Order and Constancy in the Educational Process in General Schools of the German Democratic Republic" (the so-called Lange Decree of February 12, 1958):

1.

(1)   The organs of education are charged with taking measures to abolish the immoderate extra-school demands made on pupils.

(2)   Any extra-school demands on the pupil may be made only

---

[40] Otto Dibelius, *Grenzen des Staates* (Tübingen: Furche-Verlag, 1949), p. 95.

after the completion of curricular instruction and other obligatory activities of the school; a suitable interval must intervene during which the children can recover their physical and mental powers. Any extra-curricular activities may only take place if an interval of at least two hours intervenes between them and the ending of curricular instruction.

3.

(1) Any person instructing or educating the pupils outside the curriculum or outside the school must be suitable for this responsible task. They must have a positive attitude to the Workers' and Farmers' State. Decision as to admission of such persons—insofar as they are not state-employed teachers or educators—is the responsibility of the school head. Only nationals of the German Democratic Republic are to be admitted.

(2) Persons admitted receive a certificate, the validity of which is renewable quarterly by the school head. Admittance may be revoked at any time.

5.

Recruiting with a view to participation in religious instruction is prohibited in schools and their institutions. Insofar as under Para. 1 rooms for religious instruction of pupils are made available such instruction may only proceed for the period of compulsory elementary education.

6.

The school head is responsible for strict adherence to this ordinance and to this end shall examine all extra-school and other extra-curricular activities as to form and content and to check the activity of the persons entrusted with the activities.[41]

There are no limits to the control granted in such supervision. It is clear that the actual intent is to keep children from any religious instruction. The prescribed two-hour interval between regular instruction and religious instruction necessitates a second trip to school, which is not only discouraging for the child but is often completely impossible. If instruction is to be planned for Satur-

---

[41] *The Evangelical Church in Berlin and the Soviet Zone of Germany,* trans. Patrick Lynch (Berlin: Eckart Verlag, 1959), p. 34.

days or Sundays, activities of the state youth organizations often render these hours unavailable. Still Article 44 of the Constitution of the German Democratic Republic guarantees freedom of religious instruction in the schools:

> The right of the Church to administer religious instruction in the rooms of schools is guaranteed. The religious instruction will be administered by persons selected by the Church. No person may be forced to administer or be prevented from administering religious instruction. The legal guardians of the pupils shall decide as to participation in religious instruction.[42]

The opportunity to receive instruction in the Christian faith is, indeed, still present, but the most powerful forces in education are at work to render Christianity superfluous—as, indeed, it is understood to be—rather than to promote it. Beginning in kindergarten the younger generation is taught that its supreme loyalty is to the state. When the Christian faith is made to appear contemptible, when freedom of religion is understood as tolerance of private religious opinion and freedom of worship, when religious instruction is confined to the home and public worship, and when the highly gifted children of Christian parents, and particularly church workers, are denied entrance to the technical schools and universities, Christian faith must be slowly strangled. In addition, the construction of new churches is hindered, and all the machinery of the state and its organizations, the press, films, radio, theatre, law, welfare work, and youth activities serve to promote the ideology of dialectical materialism. The influence of the church must inevitably decrease when the youth are alienated from it. When the avenues of culture are blocked in this way, the church is condemned to a slow death. It will be starved out by financial measures and by its dearth of pastors just as surely as the opponents of Communism are starved out physically.

In Communist countries a close bond is cultivated between

---

[42] *Ibid.*, p. 35; original text given in *Kirchliches Jahrbuch* (1955), p. 291.

schools and the society for which they prepare. Schools are attached to factories and learning is coordinated with productive labor. Young people are brought to see and experience the cooperative, complementary character of each segment in society far more than in the West.

There is a battle for the minds of the young going on behind the Iron Curtain. But a similar, if less spectacular, battle is being waged for the schools in America today. The proposal has frequently been made that all American children attend a state-sponsored school system; the slogan "Every Child in a Public School" expresses this idea quite succinctly. The intentions of many of its advocates may be praiseworthy, but the effect would be to reduce the rich and desirable diversity provided by parochial and private schools to a state-serving, monolithic uniformity. For some advocates, at least, of a single school system its outstanding prerogative would be the promotion of social unification; by promoting this end the public school would be more "genuinely religious" than are the schools which teach unintelligible dogmas.[43] Not a few disciples of John Dewey have presented cogent and thoughtful apologies for his stand on the religious character of democracy and the public schools. Mrs. Agnes Meyer has been one of the most outspoken. For her the public school is the great vehicle of mutual love, forgiveness, and tolerance between creeds, classes, and races.[44] It can develop morality and strengthen character in a way the Christian churches have failed to do. Some years ago James B. Conant joined the attack on the private school as "divisive" in a democracy.[45] The schools, he claimed, are the "new engines of democracy." There should be a single system of education which would mold all elements of the population into a harmonious,

[43] John Dewey, *Intelligence in the Modern World* (New York: Modern Library, 1939), pp. 713-14.

[44] Agnes Meyer, "The Clerical Challenge to the Schools," *The Atlantic Monthly*, March, 1952, pp. 42-46.

[45] James B. Conant, "The Threat of the Private School," *Saturday Review*, May 3, 1952, pp. 11-14.

democratic unity. Independent schools, including especially those operated under religious auspices, cannot be consonant with the formation of a democratic order. The National Education Association has entered this debate, too, in what Dr. Sterling McMurrin has described, in his comments on the N.E.A. upon resigning as Commissioner of Education, as a "pathological opposition to the parochial schools." These forces appear to be winning in their efforts to make the American public schools the confessional schools of democracy.

4

NEW SYMBOLS FOR NEW VALUES

> CHRISTIANITY—*and this is its fairest merit—sub-dued to a certain extent the brutal warrior ardour of the Germans, but it did not entirely quench it; and when the cross, that restraining talisman, falls to pieces, then will break forth again the ferocity of the old combatants, the frantic Berserker rage whereof Northern poets have said and sung so much. The talisman has become rotten, and the day will come when it will pitifully crumble to dust. The old stone gods will then arise from the forgotten ruins and wipe from their eyes the dust of centuries and Thor with his giant hammer will arise again, and he will shatter the Gothic ca-thedrals.*
>
> HEINRICH HEINE, *Religion and Philosophy in Germany* (1835)

Man is, as Ernst Cassirer has emphasized, the *animal symboli-cum*.[1] Whether in speech, art, or vast social schemes, men are al-ways constructing symbolic structures about themselves by which they may interpret the physical world and events. The symbol is a phenomenon meaningful in itself, but it also points beyond it-self to another and distinct meaning. This "pointing beyond" is rooted in an intrinsic relationship between symbol and the reality it discloses. The word "symbol," from the Greek *symbolon* ("token"), derives from the practice of concluding agreements by breaking a bone or some other object and giving each party to the agreement one of the broken pieces, one of the "symbols." Wherever the symbol is carried it retains its relation to the other part, and thus can witness to its own identity and to that of the person who presents it. Through the specific symbol something

---

[1] *Essay on Man* (New Haven: Yale University Press, 1944), pp. 25-26.

inclusive and universal is suggested. It establishes a relationship of trust and a proof of identity. This relationship is not based purely on arbitrary or accidental features, as is the case with a sign. Within the Christian scheme of things the reality of the true symbol is always related in some way to God himself. The power the symbol possesses is always, in the last analysis, God's power. In the political ideologies the emotions aroused—of cherishing, despising, or revering—become the dominant considerations.

Modern Symbols and Consolidation of Group Identity

The multiplicity of meanings clustering about a great economic, political, or national movement are never crystal-clear. They are ambiguous, and they are shared by very few. So the symbol is always necessary in order to make events intelligible to others. In a flash it suggests a pattern synthesizing a thousand disparate features. Thus the successful symbol will be concrete, unifying, and appealing to many backgrounds of experience. *Mein Kampf* offered, but first of all it *was,* an explanation of untold, nameless suffering. Like other great symbols it acquired a mystical significance: it was not so important for its narrative and argument as for the fact that it precluded all argument and made argument unnecessary. Thus the symbol furnishes a framework with which to probe meanings and inject order into the chaos of objects and events. Without it we would be powerless to deal constructively with the complexity of our experience.

Moreover, the symbol is required to consolidate the loyalties of dissimilar or competing groups. It binds groups together on the basis of acceptance of the same symbol. *Mein Kampf* provided a center of meaning for individuals and groups in Germany who had no other cohesive center to which to turn. In ancient religious usage the swastika symbolized the sun or cosmic unity,[2] but in Nazi Germany it represented the unity and power of the New Order. Émile Durkheim pointed this out in the case of primitive

---

[2] Cf. Jörg Lechler, *Vom Hakenkreuz: die Geschichte eines Symbols* (Leipzig: Curt Kabitzsch Verlag, 1934), pp. 7 ff.

ritual; he saw nothing in religion beyond the collective representations of the group: his general conclusion was that religion is
something eminently social. Religious representations are collective representations which express collective realities; religious rites
are a manner of acting which takes rise in the midst of the assembled groups and which is destined to excite, maintain, or re-
create certain mental states in these groups.[3]

The role of symbols in such advanced societies as Italy, Germany, and America indicates that symbols are not a feature of an
early, relatively undeveloped society. They operate in the most
highly developed societies and, indeed, are even more necessary to
reinforce the coherence of disunited groups. Here, too, they function to reinforce the group identity. The symbol reassures the individual of the existence of the group and provides him with a
means of identifying himself ever and again with this larger group.
The symbol provides a sense of direction and purpose.

Moreover, because of their function in binding people together,
symbols become cues for common action.[4] By capturing the symbols available to people a political party can capture their basic
beliefs and incite them to courageous and determined action. Common actions are possible against the background of common symbols.

The symbols discussed here bear an obvious and characteristic
relationship to the great religious faiths which earlier nourished
the cultures in which the symbols live on. Repeatedly one finds
that Christian rites and symbols are not discarded as outworn or
irrelevant. Though they lose their specific Christian content they
still recall the ultimate reality to which they once pointed. They
live a stunted form of life. They are reinterpreted as bearers of
a new reality; through them men share in the palpable activity of

[3] Émile Durkheim, *The Elementary Forms of the Religious Life,* trans. Joseph Ward Swain (Glencoe, Ill.: The Free Press, 1947), p. 10.
[4] Cf. Richard McKeon, "Symbols, Myths, and Arguments," *Symbols and
Values: An Initial Study,* ed. Lyman Bryson *et al.* (New York: Harper and
Brothers, 1954), pp. 22-26.

the nation rather than in the divine activity. Paul Tillich's insights into the viability of symbols deserve attention here:

> . . . symbols cannot be replaced at will; they must be interpreted as long as they are alive. . . . The theologian cannot give a judgment concerning the life or death of the symbols he interprets. This judgment occurs in the consciousness of the living church and has deep roots in the collective unconscious. It happens in the liturgical realm, in personal devotion, in preaching and in teaching, in the activities of the church toward the world, and in the quiet contemplation of its members.[5]

The National Socialist Reinterpretation

In view of their revolutionary reorganization of society, the ideologies must infuse language, too, with radically new meanings. Words gain new associations and connotations. Those who hear or read these words scarcely realize that they have acquired new clusters of meaning. Through their appropriation of such terms as *gottgläubig* ("god fearing"), *positives Christentum* ("positive Christianity"), and *entkonfessionalisiert* ("non-denominational"), the Nazis attempted to confuse people and thus to allay suspicions and to capture old loyalties. Such terms possessed a hallowed ring, and few suspected the designs behind the uses to which the Nazis put them. The Nazis were purifying the Christian religion. Yet Hitler's own cynicism had dissolved all Christian beliefs:

> Hitler did not believe in a personal god. He believed only in the bond of blood between succeeding generations and in a vague conception of fate or providence. Nor did he believe in a life after death. In this connection he often quoted a sentence from the *Edda*, that remarkable collection of ancient Icelandic literature, which to him represented the profoundest Nordic wisdom: "All things will pass away, nothing will remain but death and the glory of deeds."[6]

On the one hand, the Nazis pretended to disdain "churchly"

---

[5] *Systematic Theology* (2 vols.; Chicago: The University of Chicago Press, 1957), II, 165.

[6] Walter Schellenberg, *The Labyrinth*, trans. Louis Hagen (New York: Harper and Brothers, 1956), p. 94.

forms as dead in contrast to the strong, new German faith. In keeping with this claim they removed portraits of saints and crucifixes from churches and homes. The celebration of Christmas was reinterpreted as the Winter Solstice Celebration, the festival marking the renaissance of a latently powerful people. Following are the rubrics for the Winter Solstice Festival as it was to be celebrated by the *Sturmabteilung* (S.A.), the brown-shirted storm troops of the Nazi movement:

The Storm Troops *(Stürme)* march silently to the site of the celebration, usually an elevation. An immense swastika stands out in the sky, visible for many miles.

The celebration begins with the pledge to the banners. After this a verse from a combat song resounds. Meanwhile the fire flares forth mightily, illumines the banners of the movement, and announces this German celebration to everyone. Then the Storm Leader says:

"When men stand together in this sacred night and find themselves at the blazing fire, they wish to demonstrate that they are of one faith, that they bear love in their hearts for their people, and that they are willing to fight for the rebirth of the light.

"However, we recognize, too, on this day of solstice that the decision falls here in the battle between light and darkness, between good and evil, between Yes and No.

"We know that, bound up with the victory of this new light, is the decay of that false faith. We know that our faith will make our people strong in its fight for life.

"In this holy hour we become aware of the bloodstream of our ancestors. It becomes clear to us in this hour that as children of our forefathers and as ancestors of generations to come we bear an enormous responsibility, that we must preserve our inheritance that it may not perish and that it may be passed on undiminished into the eternity of the people. We believe in the trinity of body, soul, and spirit. For us death is nothing; the life of the people is everything. Our prayer is work for this people. All our love belongs to this people. Our hatred belongs to its enemy.

"We know that in our faith we follow the laws of God and are for that reason truly god-fearing *(gottgläubig)* men. Here in this sacred hour of the year's solstice we wish to swear that with a fanatical will we want to impress this faith upon our people that it may become free. We wish to vow here that in life and in death we will follow the Führer, who has brought us this redeeming faith. In this hour we are glad, for it gives us hope in the coming light, in coming victory. However, we could not rejoice at this time were we not to remember those who once gave their lives in order that the German people might live eternally."

Three SA men, three Hitler youth, and three men from the workers corps each throw into the fire a wreath for "heroes of war," "eternal vigilance," and "the offering of our daily bread." Then someone speaks the festive closing words: "Set the torches afire and carry them as signs of the reborn light through the sacred night *{Weihenacht}*, that they may set aflame the hearts of all who believe in the banner. To Adolf Hitler, who raised this banner into the light and saved Germany, we vow loyalty and faithfulness."[7]

Nazi rites and symbols showed a certain arbitrary character as they appeared in rapid succession from the Office for Cultural Affairs. But by the time of the collapse in 1945 Himmler's SS constituted a powerful cultic organization with a consistently articulated world-view.[8] It was planned as the model for the entire Nazi development. Himmler's ideal was the structure, education, and discipline of the Jesuit Order, which appear to have exerted a decisive attraction on both Hitler and Himmler.[9] Hitler was always aware of the effect on the populace of vivid and forceful deeds. Through their singular content these deeds became means for further, greater deeds.[10] The Nazi rites were the religious consecration of politics. They celebrated events sacred to the nascent nation, for example, the passage of heroic life and purpose to the newborn infant, the holy union of man and woman as co-workers in the national community. No churchly rite or divine grace was necessary to "make holy" what had been binding on German blood already from antiquity.[11]

---

[7] *SA-Mann,* No. 1 (January 2, 1937).

[8] The extent to which the SS was the cultic comradeship of a common idea is revealed in *Die Feier* and in the issues of *Die neue Gemeinschaft.*

[9] Cf. Schellenberg, *op. cit.*

[10] Cf. Hannah Arendt, *The Origins of Totalitarianism,* pp. 301 ff.

[11] Cf. Wilhelm Hauer, *Germany's New Religion* (New York: Abingdon Press, 1937), pp. 56 ff.

But the symbols of the secular cults uniformly show a contrived and self-conscious character better adapted to the sophisticated, rational mind than to the naïve, primitive mentality. Primary interest is always directed toward the impressions created, toward the mental state invoked in the participants. Such symbols as the swastika and hammer and sickle reveal the conscious attempt to create a serviceable symbol; they lack organic growth in history. The masses, however, do not perceive this: they are led to believe the symbols have arisen from historical experience. There is a dramatic character to the symbols; they evoke strong sentiment and unify a group. The spiritual *mana* here resides in the social group.

Christian faithful, on the other hand, have always pointed to the historical character of the events commemorated in their creeds. The cross points beyond itself to the central sacrifice on Calvary. The sacraments are traced to institution by Christ. The painstaking, scholarly investigation into biblical sources is a historical preoccupation. There are, to be sure, philosophical, sociological, and psychological considerations with respect to Christian signs and symbolic acts. But the crucial questions emerge again and again as historical issues. What Gerhard Kittel wrote regarding the relation of Christianity to the ancient mysteries applies also to the ideologies:

> The Gospel of Christ crucified is utterly unmythical. It is not a song and not a strain of music, and not an idea, and not a myth or a symbol. It does not speak of remote legend, but of an immediately near, realistic, brutal, wretched, and terrible episode of history. . . . The terrible realism of the Cross is softened by no patina of age and by no aesthetics. . . . Beautiful and profound ideas, secret magic, mystery—all this was as well or better known to other religions than to early Christianity. If their believers gave heed to the message of Christ, they did so because it was a perfectly realistic message.[12]

[12] *Die Religionsgeschichte und das Urchristentum,* pp. 124 ff.; quoted by Hugo Rahner, "The Christian Mysteries and the Pagan Mysteries," in *Pagan and Christian Mysteries,* ed. Joseph Campbell (New York: Harper Torchbooks, 1963), pp. 168-69.

Another aspect of Christianity which sets it apart from the rites of the ideologies is its message of redemption from sin by God's grace. The modern nature-ideologies recognize no radical disruption, no all-embracing need on the part of a fallen humanity, and consequently no comparable restoration or remission. As strongly as Christianity emphasizes man's alienation from the light and life of God, so it stands or falls on its appeal to the grace of God present in the incarnate Son.[13]

Heroes and Secular Saviors

Primitive peoples ascribed a magical potency to their leaders, who were regarded as possessing special *charismata*. In distinction from symbolic persons these leaders exuded unusual charismatic gifts which attracted and fascinated their followers. Egyptian pharaohs simply declared themselves to be gods incarnate, so that at Abu Simbel the god Osiris is represented on the Osirian pillars with the features of Rameses II. Asian kings represented themselves as agents of the gods, and even Alexander the Great employed religion as a cloak for his growing absolutism. He professed to believe in his own divinity and sent orders to the Greek city-states that he be accorded divine honors.

The modern leader assumes the form of the savior or redeemer from economic and political ills. It was no accident that Mussolini took the title *Il Duce* and Hitler wanted no greater honor than to be named *Der Führer*.[14] Both men were heirs of Caesar and, like Caesar, both nurtured a Caesar myth.

Lenin's teacher, Plekhanov, wrote a famous treatise on *The Role of the Individual in History*.[15] Here Plekhanov ascribes the "great

---

[13] Cf. Hugo Rahner, *op. cit.*, pp. 170-71.

[14] See the discussion of charismatic leadership in Hans H. Gerth's essay, "The Nazi Party: Its Leadership and Composition," *Reader in Bureaucracy,* ed. Robert K. Merton, Ailsa P. Gray, Barbara Hockey, Hanan C. Selvin (Glencoe, Ill.: The Free Press, 1952), pp. 100 ff. Gerth quotes Hermann Göring: ". . . We National Socialists believe . . . that for us the Leader is . . . simply infallible" (p. 101).

[15] Moscow: Foreign Language Publishing House, 1944.

man" to the "surface" of history: in the final analysis it is not personality but the social forces of time which determine events. Lenin, while maintaining the orthodox Marxist dogma of social determinism, made allowances for a more distinctive role of the leader in directing the revolutionary masses. The portraits of Marx and Lenin in Russia and the satellite countries suggest something closer to Thomas Carlyle's view of the place of the hero in history. The "cult of personality" is closer to Carlyle's paeans to the creative personality than to Plekhanov's sober determinism.

In Russia as well as in other countries men and movements have needed heroes. For centuries Russia had lived on the myth of the czar, of the God-sent ruler, whose actions could not be judged by human standards. By the time of the Bolshevik revolution in 1917 this myth was in eclipse; the slaughter of "Bloody Sunday" had contributed much to this. But the czar myth, so deeply rooted in the Russian consciousness, has been carried over under new names.[16]

Lenin himself, so potent both as myth and symbol, has proved to be the most durable of Communist demi-gods. In a sense he still exercises his *charismata:* his inspired writings, the legends surrounding his activities, and the museums preserving his memory all bespeak his immortality.[17] He is used to sanctify past decisions and to legitimize doctrinal and practical innovations; the slogan "Back to Lenin" has become the rallying point for the most divergent interests. Russian peasants had venerated their czar as the "Little Father," but in the czar's place stepped Lenin as personal father symbol.[18] Lenin, Eisenhower, Adenauer were new "fathers" of their countries—partly because of the insecurities of the contemporary world. President Eisenhower was accorded, or allowed to acquire, a divinity reminiscent of medieval kings. General Mac-

[16] Cf. Michael Cherniavsky, *Tsar and People* (New Haven: Yale University Press, 1961), *passim.*

[17] Cf. Dinko Tomasic, *The Impact of Russian Culture on Soviet Communism* (Glencoe, Ill.: The Free Press, 1953), pp. 207 ff.

[18] Cf. William O. Douglas, *Russian Journey* (Garden City: Doubleday and Co., 1956), p. 61.

Arthur, too, with his keen sense of destiny and of the ritual of high military office, played out the role of modern hero.[19] Unnamed and indefinable fears haunt the average soldier and citizen. He will hardly search for the source of these fears, but he will invoke many centers of security. MacArthur, very much like De Gaulle, became the symbol of confidence: his own calmness and mastery of situations inspired similar responses in his followers. In the rock of Mount Rushmore the faces of the authentic American saints have been perpetuated. Lincoln, especially, is seen by many Americans as the symbol of self-sacrifice. He laid down his life for equality and unity. He was common in his tastes but resplendent in his virtues. He has been elevated by many Americans to the rank of a demi-god, similar to the savior-gods of the Hellenistic world.

To be sure, the orthodox will disclaim the comparison, but a practical infallibility has been ascribed Marx and Lenin which makes papal infallibility seem a half-hearted compromise. In the November 7 and May Day parades in the squares of Moscow and Peking heroes from a new Olympus make their ceremonial appearances; they choose their sides in the affairs of men. Here the party hierarchies, ranged in ceremonial order at the navel centers of their worlds, review the symbolic expressions of their military power. A parallel is apparent here to the ancient emperors of Rome seated in the proscenium.[20]

Leningrad, Stalingrad, Karl Marx Stadt, and many other cities have been renamed to honor new heroes. In late 1961 Premier Nikita Khrushchev's sweeping de-Stalinization program suddenly took on momentum. A number of important changes were made. Stalin's embalmed body was peremptorily demoted from the mausoleum in Red Square. The "hero city" on the Volga River, Stalingrad, known as Tsaritsyn before the Bolsheviks made tsars

---

[19] Cf. James Michener, *The Voice of Asia* (New York: Random House, 1951).

[20] See Helmut Gollwitzer's discussion of the cult of the great man in history, *Unwilling Journey*, p. 154.

unpopular, received the more neutral name Volgograd. Stalinsk, the steel city in southern Siberia, regained its old name Novokuznetsk, and Stalino, the Ukrainian mining town, has become Donetsk. In East Germany the steel show city of Stalinstadt has become Eisenhüttenstadt. Dozens of Stalin streets, squares, factories, institutes, and establishments have been renamed, and the late dictator's name is being lost to heroic history.[21]

Martin Luther University in Halle, East Germany, was renamed for a new reformer: it is now Walter Ulbricht University. In 1953 Leipzig University was renamed Karl Marx University. Martin Luther's role as the great German reformer has been systematically combated through the promotion of another sixteenth century reformer, Thomas Müntzer. Müntzer is lauded for his interest in dissolving class differences and for his espousal of a new ordering of society. By his violent uprooting of established orders he is said to be the precursor of the Communist revolution in the revolt against feudalism.

In Communist countries today the cult of work is taking the place of the cult of Christian worship; folk heroes, in the form of the Activist, or "hero of labor," are replacing the Christian saints. Such heroes become symbolic persons: they represent the possibilities of human perfection within a Socialist society. They are normative images of self-realization and self-fulfillment. In many Russian cities today statues of groups of workers have replaced the discarded statues of Stalin. China's Communists have given these labor heroes great "face" through such means as widespread publicity, special benefits, and free trips to Europe. A recent visitor to China describes viewing an old temple on the hills overlooking the Yangtze south of Langchow. Written on its walls in giant characters was the statement: "The heroes of yesterday are dead. The heroes of today are at work."[22] The workers are the Hercu-

---

[21] Even the famous "Socialist" street of East Berlin, the Stalinallee, has become Frankfurter Allee.

[22] Gerard Destanne de Bernis, "What I Saw in Red China," *Catholic World*, January, 1960, p. 233.

lean demi-gods of the New Society. They are celebrated for their divine deeds. Note the poem entitled "Workers" by a worker poet of Shanghai, which bears the stamp of Psalm 46:

> We stamp our feet, and the earth trembles;
> We blow a breath, and the roaring river makes way;
> We lift our hands, and mighty mountains shiver;
> We stride forward, and none dare block our path.
> We are the workers—our strength is invincible.[23]

International Communism has its martyrs and confessors in many lands, but the martyrdom of Karl Liebknecht and Rosa Luxemburg in Berlin on January 15, 1919, has a significance for the entire Communist movement. They were the undeceived leaders of early Socialism. They had been snatched from their followers by bestial monopolists and warmongers. They offered themselves in the struggle for a better life for the worker. Their spiritual descendants can say, "These two upright people, fighters for the German working class, should be prototypes for all of us and especially for our youth. In their spirit we wish to fight against war and hatred for a united, democratic, peace-loving Germany. For this we are indebted to these two great dead."[24]

We have seen that the *Führerprinzip* formed an essential element in Nazi ideology. A living hero was required at that particular juncture of world events to lead Germany from political and economic blundering. Hitler became the great savior-leader with whom the rank and file of the German population could identify themselves. Their weakness was taken up in his strength. Soldiers at the front could continue to resist or die because of their identification with the Führer.[25] The meaning of the struggle

---

[23] "The People's Poetry," *The Atlantic Monthly,* December, 1959, p. 94.

[24] "Zum Gedenken Karl Liebknechts und Rosa Luxemburgs," *Heimatbote des Kreises Greis,* V, 1 (January, 1959), 5.

[25] Cf. "Primary Groups in the German Army," abridged and adapted in Leonard Broom and Philip Selznick, *Sociology* (2nd ed.; Evanston: Row, Peterson and Co., 1958), p. 149.

so clearly envisaged by him became their meaning. He had "redeemed" Germany from internal dissension and alien controls; because of his racial blood-unity with the German people he was at once the "mouthpiece" of their spirit and their representative. Eric Voegelin compares the relationship with a biblical precedent: "The *Führer* is the point at which the spirit of the people breaks into historical reality; the inner-worldly God speaks to the *Führer* in the same way as the other-worldly God spoke to Abraham, and the *Führer* transforms the divine words into a commandment for the narrower discipleship and for the people."[26] The Führer was even named the "Son of God," the one who, by his presence among the German people, made them aware of their divine sonship. He revealed this great awareness to his brethren by his marvelous deeds.[27]

To the very last days of the war new wonders were awaited from Hitler. Children were taught to fold their hands, bow their heads, and devoutly thank their Führer, "who gives us work and bread, helps us in our every need."[28] Expectant mothers voiced a similar blessing over their abundant food. With their right hand raised, facing Hitler's huge portrait, they confessed, "Our *Führer,* we thank thee for thy munificence; we thank thee for this home; we thank thee for this food. To thee we devote all our powers; to thee we dedicate our lives and those of our children!"[29] A variation on this procedure reveals the sole mediation of the Führer even more dramatically. The *Sturmbahnführer* of the SA called out the words, "Der Führer," after a moment's silence when all

---

[26] *Die politischen Religionen* (Stockholm: Bermann-Fischer Verlag, 1939), pp. 57-8.

[27] Cf. F. W. Woweries, *Schulungsbrief der NSDAP und DAF,* III, 12 (December, 1936). The *Schulungsbrief* was issued monthly by the education office *(Reichsschulungsamt)* of the Nazi party (NSDAP) and the German Labor Front *(Deutsche Arbeitsfront).* An official publication distributed to German school teachers, it was also made available to members of the party and of the Labor Front and to the army.

[28] Romano Guardini, *Der Heilbringer in Mythus, Offenbarung, und Politik* (Stuttgart: Deutsche Verlags-Anstalt, 1946), p. 42.

[29] Gregor Ziemer, *Education for Death: The Making of the Nazi* (New York: Oxford University Press, 1941), p. 34.

the men had gathered for their noon-day meal. And all responded quietly and festively, "Der Führer."[30]

The essential nature of German nationalism required an appeal to heroic German antiquity. Arminius, defender of German soil against Roman encroachment under Caesar Augustus, and Duke Widukind, the marshal of Saxon arms against Charlemagne's alien culture, became the forebears of Reichsführer Adolph Hitler. In 1934, at the revival of the pagan festival of the summer solstice, Alfred Rosenberg planted a memorial grove to Duke Widukind's memory. In the Third Reich the entire pantheon of Wagnerian gods was called upon to perform a cultic function.

But there were also martyrs and confessors. There were the early martyrs who were cut down before the Feldherrnhalle in Munich on November 9, 1923. Hitler dedicated the first volume of *Mein Kampf* to them as the "blood witnesses" of this event: "may they shine forever, a glowing example to the followers of our movement."[31] They had "sacrificed themselves for us all with the clearest consciousness. They must forever recall the wavering and the weak to the fulfillment of his duty, a duty which they themselves in the best faith carried to its final consequence."[32] Annual rites honored their memory; the youngest, Karl La Force, became the object of special veneration. Following is a document describing Nazism's honoring of its heroes, as outlined by a Nazi leader in an address at Blaubeuren:

Our primary experience is of our Führer Adolf Hitler, who stems from the primeval depths of the people. Thereupon we call to mind our ancestors and our history, which is transmitted through the idea of blood. The individual person is swallowed up in his people and his state. And every man of German blood is capable of this experience in some form or other, each according to his own manner. The only thing needed is cultivation and schooling, and then the German

[30] "Neues Leben im Schloss, das einst Rom gehörte," *Völkischer Beobachter,* November 14, 1936.

[31] *Mein Kampf,* trans. Ralph Manheim (Boston: Houghton Mifflin, 1943), "Dedication."

[32] *Ibid.,* p. 687.

man is saved. Then the German people will master the future. It is from this experience that the idea, nature, and realization of National Socialism first arise. The decisive work for the beginning as well as for the end of this achievement is the Führer's work *Mein Kampf,* whose riches future generations will be unable to exhaust. The Führer's speeches furnish ever new experiences and ever new and clear insights; our generation has the great good fortune to be able to learn from the Führer himself. Following the idea comes the emergence of cultic expressions, the fixed form in which the meaning of the world-view is vibrant. Just as the church gradually created its cultic structure, so in its festivals National Socialism gives birth to visible cultic forms capable of stirring the emotions. The first of May has already become an established festival, one which rouses the entire people and to which they look forward. On June 24 [the summer solstice] we light flames of life for the festival of youth and for the eternity of the people. The *Party Day* annually becomes a mighty testimony of power and annually gathers the people together in a mighty testimony of power, annually gathers the faithful for a grand roll call. The *Day of the Farmer,* the peoples' harvest festival, can just as little be erased from the list of the peoples' rites. In addition to these, there comes each year on November 9 the *Day of Heroes.* The death of the men at the Feldherrnhalle is something so singular and unusual that this occurrence should actually stand at the beginning of the [Nazi] world-view as an everlasting event; these men guaranteed the future of the movement for us. It was no mournful procession which passed through the streets of Munich, but a triumphal procession of resurrection, a staggering and inspiring experience, an apotheosis with which the movement thanked its dead. The public buildings in Munich which breathe their spirit exceed in power and significance everything that this city of architectural excellence has yet produced. They are the symbol of the might and victorious power of an idea. The Temple of Honor at its center dedicated to "eternal vigilance" signifies beginning as well as end. And it is nothing other than the achievement of an entirely new cultic form when the names of the martyrs are called forth and the thousand-fold "Hier" resounds, testifying to the continuing life of the spirit of those who demonstrated by their death the march into life. This is not a matter of cold understanding, but an experience no one can forget. Whoever has made it a part of himself will never betray the sixteen dead. So something occurs which one may call rite and the shaping of a tradition: the transmission of the new spirit to the entire people. Thus we sense: Adolf Hitler becomes Germany, he has the power to reshape the German people, to give sixty million people a new attitude. He lifts the soul on high. The further development of this experience in spirit and attitude, in form and action, cannot be halted; it is destined to continue for millennia to come. There is nothing like it on the face of the earth.[33]

The day of a hero's death was celebrated in Hitler's Germany as the day of his transfiguration. He was to be commemorated, in his nobler, transformed existence, in the circle of the party and by his close relatives. Themes and representative personalities were assigned as well to particular months. For example, Frederick the Great was remembered in January for his military achievements and for his struggle to establish Prussian hegemony. Fichte was feted in May as the great philosopher of the wars of freedom; Freiherr von Stein was celebrated in October as the great German social reformer.[34] All of these heroes were the distinguished representatives of the German attitude toward destiny. They were important instruments for educating the young; they supplied the adolescent's need for impelling models after which to pattern their lives.

Sacred Space: National Shrines and Pilgrimages

Living heroes have a habit of becoming dead saints. A canonization procedure forms a feature of each of the great national cults. A conception of "real presence" is preserved for those who make their pilgrimage to these sacred shrines. The site is uniformly a

[33] *Blaubeurener Tageblatt,* November 14, 1935. Reprinted in Karl Immer, *Entchristlichung der Jugend; Eine Materialsammlung* (Wuppertal-Barmen: Verlag Unter dem Wort, 1936), pp. 21-22.

[34] Cf. *Weltanschauliche Feierstunden der NSDAP* (Munich: Franz Eher, 1944), p. 8. In accordance with a directive from Reichsleiter Arnold Rosenberg these hours, which were designed to transmit a communal experience of National Socialism, were to take place on the *same* day, at the *same* hour, and, wherever possible, in *each* and *every* district (*ibid.*, pp. 7 ff.). The importance of each local party group's having its own festive room—one might almost say "place of worship"—is emphasized also in *Die Gestaltung der Lebensfeiern,* p. 13.

natural or man-made mound or mountain—Hitler's *Feierstätte*, or "cultic sites," dotted many historic hills and preempted many a historic castle. The embalmed body best evokes the presence of the unique, dynamic personality, as in the case of Lenin and Eva Peron. They are not risen, neither are they wholly dead. But the solitary sarcophagus is almost equally effective when given a mausoleum of heroic proportions. A grateful Turkey could be depended upon to perform this honor for Ataturk, but General Franco was not willing to leave his immortality to the shifting memories of men. A shrine for the dictator is being completed outside Madrid, and the Christian character of his state is to be preserved by the religious services to be held there daily. In this respect he is continuing the traditions of the earlier pantheons, of the twelfth century Cistercian monastery at Poblet and of Phillip II's ambitious El Escorial near Madrid.

It is not surprising that one should find impressive national shrines developed as a matter of national policy. Islam has its Kaaba at Mecca, Christianity its shrines in the Holy Land and the Eternal City. Pious Moslems and Christians hope to visit these once during their lifetime. A mystic lure attracts the modern Russian to the Kremlin and to the numinous presence in the Lenin mausoleum. For millions of Russians the aspiration of Chekhov's *Sisters* must draw them on, "To Moscow! Moscow! Moscow!" A queue of pilgrims from all over the Soviet Union waits to pay devotion to these remains. Some are drawn by curiosity, others are following an acceptable behavior pattern; but for others it assumes sacred rather than purely secular overtones.[35] The memory of the "immortal" Lenin, founder of the Communist Party and of the Soviet Union, is perpetuated here, while the remains of "mortal" Stalin have been removed. Frequently groups of young "Pioneers," similar to our Boy Scouts and Girl Scouts, are taken to the mausoleum for their initiation. The line in the square is often more

---

[35] Cf. John Gunther, *Inside Russia Today* (New York: Harper and Brothers, 1957), pp. 32-33.

than half a mile long. Each year there are millions of visitors at the shrine. The ceremonial significance of this martyr's grave is only accentuated by the existence of an exact duplicate at Ulan Bator in Outer Mongolia.

The conflict of loyalties between Christian and secular shrines is dramatized in the struggle over the great church of St. Genevieve, patron saint of Paris. On three occasions it has been secularized and transformed to become the Pantheon, the mausoleum containing the bodies of such illustrious Frenchmen as Voltaire, Rousseau, and Victor Hugo. Although it has been reconsecrated during the interim periods it now appears destined to remain a great national shrine.

A similar struggle has been waged in Poland, where Communist faith faces a fervent, traditional Roman Catholicism. Here the shrine of the "Black Madonna" at Yasna Gora is the center of an ancient loyalty, while the Warsaw Party Congress is the center of another. In terms of leadership the conflict revolves about the personalities of Polish Cardinal Wyszynski and party chief Gomulka.

The monumental could not be ignored by the great national religions, though one can say that the Fascist glorification of the state has made it particularly amenable to magnificent public works. When Peron was overthrown, Buenos Aires faced an embarrassing problem in its partially completed monuments. The Fascist monuments standing unfinished outside Rome match the proportions of ancient Roman buildings, while the Palace of the Knights of St. John which Mussolini restored on Rhodes equals the finest medieval buildings. The plain red granite and black-gray labradorite mausoleum enclosing Lenin's remains compares favorably with the pyramids of Egypt; his tomb has its counterpart in the Cathedral of St. Basil the Beatified on the same Red Square, and the pale corpses have their counterpart in the mummified saints in the Cloister of the Caves at Kiev. By way of contrast, Hitler would not permit William I to be interred in Germany; but the tombs of the great founders of the Reich, Henry I at Quedlinburg and Henry the Lion in the "Staatsdom" at Braunschweig, were named "shrines" of the German people. They were honored and visited as "holy centers of pilgrimage" which were to proclaim the spirit and deeds of German heroes. But the glories of this world's heroes are tied to political fortunes. Today the German people must be reminded of "new" shrines. They are the chambers at Dachau and the room at Berlin-Plötzensee where the would-be assassins of July 20, 1944, were executed.

Nuremberg with its gigantic arenas planned for party congresses, the massive public works program of Mussolini in New Rome, Washington with its historic documents enshrined in helium, special glass, and reinforced concrete, all bear witness to the need for community organization about a physical symbol. Significantly, Romano Guardini has suggested that before any reality can become *"really* real" for mankind it must be located in some specific place. One must be able to point to it in space and it must endure there through time.[36] Democratic ideals are enshrined in the Declaration of Independence, the Constitution, and the Bill of Rights; they are preserved in "sacred shrines" and revered as "sacred documents." There is more than a slight danger that a religious quality of devotion may attach itself to these documents. In addition, America has innumerable shrines which pilgrims invest with sacred significance. The cemeteries of America's war dead are inviolate shrines. Here the living gather to honor the sacred memories of those who gave their lives for a supreme cause. Note the language of General John A. Logan's General Order No. 11, which instituted Memorial Day:

> The 30th day of May, 1868, is designated for the purpose of strewing with flowers or otherwise decorating the graves of comrades who died in defense of their country during the late rebellion, and whose bodies now lie in almost every city, village, hamlet, and church-yard in the land. . . .

[36] Romano Guardini, *The End of the Modern World,* trans. Joseph Themen and Herbert Burke; ed. with an introd. by Frederick D. Wilhelmsen (New York: Sheed and Ward, 1956), pp. 6-7.

We are organized, comrades, as our regulations tell us, for the purpose, among other things, "of preserving and strengthening those kind and fraternal feelings which have bound together the soldiers, sailors, and marines who united together to suppress the late rebellion." What can aid more to assure this result than by cherishing tenderly the memory of our heroic dead. . . . We should guard their graves with sacred vigilance. . . .

Let us, then, at the time appointed, gather around their sacred remains, and garland the passionless mounds above them with the choicest flowers of spring-time; let us raise above them the dear old flag they saved from dishonor; let us, in this solemn presence, renew our pledges to aid and assist those whom they have left among us. . . . [37]

Prominent among America's shrines are the birthplaces of its crises-heroes and the centers where freedom was preserved. But the tombs of its famous men stand in a class by themselves. Ralph Gabriel has described the ritual of the Lincoln Memorial as follows:

A developed cult requires a sanctuary. That of Lincoln has three—the birthplace in Kentucky, the grave in Illinois, and the great Memorial at Washington. Of these the last is the most important. Analysis reveals significant characteristics. It is a Greek temple. Within it is a graven image. John Chester French's figure is a romanticized Lincoln. Three devices enhance the religious atmosphere; on the walls in bronze are the words of the hero; a light falls from the ceiling upon his forehead; and above the brooding figure is an inscription. It reads: "In this temple as in the hearts of the people for whom he saved the Union the memory of Abraham Lincoln is enshrined forever." Hubert Work, Secretary of the Interior, called the Memorial in 1926 holy ground. In such temples and with similar inscriptions the citizens of ancient Greece placed statues of Apollo. By so little is the twentieth century after Christ separated from the fifth before His coming.

What is it that Americans worship when they stand, uncovered,

---

[37] W. Lloyd Warner, *The Living and the Dead: A Study of the Symbolic Life of Americans* ("Yankee City Series," Vol. V; New Haven: Yale University Press, 1959), pp. 261-62.

before that great, silent figure? For worship they do, more sincerely many of them, than when they occupy their pews in church. They do reverence, if one may hazard an analysis of those inarticulate emotions which put an end to loud talk and to boisterous conduct, to a personification of the American democratic faith. The phenomenon of Lincoln, Woodrow Wilson once remarked, makes it possible to believe in democracy.[38]

Lincoln as man and statesman was certainly much more than he is as symbol. As theologian he recognized man's proneness to sin, the ambiguities of decisions in the public sphere, the righteous judgment of God against all unrighteousness. He resisted the pressures to identify his ends with those of God; he would be most unhappy in his transformation into symbol.[39]

The sense of presence evoked by such shrines is attested by the ritual conducted by a troop of *Bund Deutscher Mädel* at the martyr's graves in the sacred Ehrentempel in Munich. Around the sarcophagi containing the bodies of the fourteen[40] victims of the *Putsch* of 1923 were torches burning night and day. The words engraved on the stone walls resembled a sort of secular pieta: "You have conquered after all." Gregor Ziemer reported on his visit as follows: "The leader shouted the names of the sixteen dead men, and the girls yelled back a loud 'Hier' after each name. . . . As the ceremony progressed a circle of men, women and children gathered, and joined in the shout of *Hier* until it went echoing all over the Koenigliche Platz."[41]

In each of these new shrines old religious sentiments are elicited: one finds himself alone with the sacred object, in solitary communion; a sense of awe is evoked by the monumental sur-

[38] Ralph Henry Gabriel, *The Course of American Democratic Thought: An Intellectual History since 1851* (New York: Ronald Press, 1940), pp. 412-13. Copyright © 1940 by The Ronald Press Company; used by permission of the publisher.

[39] See William J. Wolf, *The Religion of Abraham Lincoln* (New York: Seabury, 1963).

[40] The number is placed sometimes at fourteen, sometimes at sixteen.

[41] Ziemer, *op. cit.,* pp. 143-44.

roundings; one is bound to an embodied ideal in religious devotion. Ziemer describes the conclusion of the ritual as follows: "The girls were called to attention and marched to the stone coffins. They knelt down, as if they were in a cathedral, and silence settled over the square. They rose, and silently marched away; the crowd dispersed. I did not have to ask to whom these BDM *{Bund Deutscher Mädel}* girls had been praying."[42]

However, the power of the sacred place is revealed most clearly when it is snatched from the employ of one loyalty to the use of a new devotion. The ancient Greeks saw the destruction of their city as a destruction of the protecting deity standing guard over the city. Troy, Carthage, and Corinth all suffered this fate, and Athens narrowly escaped demolition through the intervention of Pallas Athena. Communist authorities have gloated over their use of the Wartburg for the Youth Dedication because a new triumph, a new power, and a new ideal could here build upon the power of an older symbolism.

Mass Meetings

It is in the great mass meetings that the collective vision of the myth is transmitted to the individual. If it is true that the ideologies grew on the soil of the isolated, uprooted mass man, it is equally true that the mass man could merge his individual identity in the collective whole and emerge sustained and soothed by an unfaltering trust.

The dedication may not be so marked as in a Billy Graham crusade, but renewed dedication is always the goal. By virtue of sheer numbers confidence is engendered and enthusiasm transmitted for an irresistible cause. The presence of the faithful becomes, in a unique sense, a witness and testimony to the truth of the cause. Adam Ulam has described the role of Moscow's party congresses as follows:

The party congresses are staged not to decide policies but to

[42] *Ibid.,* p. 144.

74

educate the rank and file of the party. The function of the delegates is to carry back to their farms, factories, and army units the reassuring picture of the united and all-powerful party and of its wise and solicitous leadership, and of "correct" and clearly elucidated policies.[43]

In the mass meeting the power of the cause, whether this be military power, moral power, or athletic prowess, is uniquely demonstrated. Communist lands have seized upon sport and youth festivals to capitalize on the infectious enthusiasm of youth, just as Mormonism has seized upon sports and youth activities in the United States and Great Britain to spread its cause. Sport and physical culture possess special significance because they symbolize the prowess which will enable workers to increase their production at the workbench, in the field, and in the lecture hall. The Socialist sport hero typifies the heroic achievement of Socialist society. From the German film *Kühle Wampe* to the World Youth Festivals, these festivals have celebrated the togetherness of young workers against common foes. In Italy today the Communist-sponsored Festival of Unity offers everything to attract the young— rock 'n' roll, games of skill and chance, wine from Communist cooperatives, a merry-go-round, and Communist doctrine.

Nazism has been interpreted very convincingly as simply an extension of the mass meeting.[44] Certainly few more spectacular meetings have taken place than the National party congresses at Nuremberg, at which half a million people participated. Hitler declared that to be a leader means to be able to move masses. At the mass meeting the leader could exercise a personal and direct influence. Hitler wrote:

The mass meeting is also necessary for the reason that in it the individual, who at first, while becoming a supporter of a young

[43] "The Displaced Mummy," *The Reporter,* November 23, 1961, p. 28. Copyright 1961 by The Reporter Magazine Company; used by permission of the author and of the publisher.

[44] Hannah Arendt, *The Origins of Totalitarianism,* pp. 310 ff., 316 ff.

movement, feels lonely and easily succumbs to the fear of being alone, for the first time gets the picture of a larger community, which in most people has a strengthening, encouraging effect . . .

. . . The man who is exposed to grave tribulations, as the first advocate of a new doctrine in his factory or workshop, absolutely needs that strengthening which lies in the conviction of being a member and fighter in a great comprehensive body. And he obtains an impression of this body for the first time in the mass demonstration. When from his little workshop or big factory, in which he feels very small, he steps for the first time into a mass meeting and has thousands and thousands of people of the same opinions around him, when, as a seeker, he is swept away by three or four thousand others into the mighty effect of suggestive intoxication and enthusiasm, when the visible success and agreement of thousands confirm to him the rightness of the new doctrine and for the first time arouse doubt in the truth of his previous conviction then he himself has succumbed to the magic influence of what we designate as "mass suggestion."[45]

The many little celebrations, the *Feierstunden* and *Weihestunden,* were lesser expressions of the one, great peoples' meeting. In all of these the solidarity of the blood-community was celebrated.

The Nazis were masters in the pageantry and ceremonial of such assemblies, but Communist rallies with their many-colored banners to emphasize the festive nature of the event have rivaled Nazi romanticism. The congress or the rally is usually dominated by some central figure or figures. In evening meetings extensive use is made of concentrated lighting, of candlelight, or torchlight parades. Music is always of singular importance in setting the mood and in eliciting enthusiasm.

Hymns and Party Songs

For the Nazis, music became the means for expressing the inner nature of their celebrations, and common song bound the celebrants into a celebrating community. Both instrumental music and

---

[45] *Mein Kampf,* pp. 478-79.

song were designed to impress the ideology on the feelings of the German people in a way that political rhetoric could never match.[46] These were directed to the "heart" rather than solely to the "head." Following is the "Song of the Hitler Jugend":

> We are the happy Hitler Youth.
> We need no Christian Virtues,
> For our Führer Adolf Hitler
> Is always our mediator.
>
> No parson, no evil man can prevent us
> From feeling ourselves Hitler children;
> We do not follow Christ but Horst Wessel,
> Away with incense and holy water vessels.
>
> We follow our flags singing
> As worthy sons of our ancestors.
> I am no Christian, no Catholic,
> I go with the SA through thick and thin.
>
> I can do without the Church.
> The Swastika is redemption on earth.
> I will dog its steps,
> Baldur von Schirach, take me with you![47]

But music, the handmaid, has allowed its strains to be used for radically differing devotions. The same melody by Franz Haydn, often sung with "Glorious Things of Thee are Spoken," rang out in the stolid "Gott erhalte unser Kaiser" and in the lusty "Deutschland, Deutschland über alles." For each of these the brass band, so much a part of traditional German festivities, has played a lead-

---

[46] Cf. *Die Gestaltung der Lebensfeiern,* p. 3.

[47] From the diary of the German Minister of Justice, p. 228; document 3751-PS, trans. in *Nazi Conspiracy and Aggression,* Office of U. S. Chief of Counsel for Prosecution of Axis Criminality (Washington: Government Printing Office, 1946), VI, 638. Horst Wessel, hailed by the Nazis as one of the martyrs of their movement, was the author of the party song, the "Horst Wessel Lied." Baldur von Schirach was the party's youth leader.

ing role, and it now invigorates the Youth Dedication and other rites.[48]

The party song may vary, but the solemn mood remains the same. Whether it is "Cara al sol" ("Face to the Sun"), "Giovinezza" of the Blackshirts, "Brüder, zur Sonne, zur Freiheit" ("Brothers, Onward to the Sun, to Freedom") of the Socialists, or the "International" of the Communist movement, the solemnity of faith appears. The sacred character of the ceremony is most apparent when the songs cease to be sung as enthusiastic combat songs and gain the character of hymns of the movement. This is the case with "The Song of the Party" by Louis Fürnberg:

> She has given us everything,
> The sun and the wind—never is she stingy.
> Wherever she was, there was life.
> Whatever we are we owe to her.
> Never has she forsaken us.
> When the world froze, we were warm,
> Protected by the mother of the masses,
> Borne up by her mighty arm.

Refrain:

> The Party, the Party is always right,
> And, comrades, so shall it ever be.
> Whoever fights for right is always right,
> Against lies and exploitation.
> Whoever outrages life is wicked or dumb.
> Whoever defends humanity is always right.
> So, nourished in the spirit of Lenin, and
>   welded together by Stalin,
> The Party, the Party, the Party.

> Never have we had her cajole us.
> Though our courage sank in the strife,
> She has only gently caressed us:
> "Fear not"—and suddenly things were all right.

[48] Cf. Appendix 2, "Basic Considerations . . . in Stalinstadt," VII.

Should we count up our sorrows and troubles,
When we succeed in gaining all good?
When for the poorest on earth
We achieve freedom and peace?

Refrain.

She has given us everything:
Bricks for building, and our great plan.
"Master your life!" she says to us.
"Forward, comrades, grab hold!"
Though hyenas incite men to war,
What you build will break their power!
So build house and build cradle!
Workers, be on your guard!

Refrain.[49]

The party possesses a practical omnipotence. These songs are sung as hymns at the atheistic rites. In the "Praise of the Party" by K. Schwaen and Bertolt Brecht something like omniscience and omnipresence is ascribed to the party:

The individual has two eyes,
The Party a thousand eyes.
The Party sees seven states,
The individual sees one city.
The individual has his hour,
But the Party many hours.
The individual can be destroyed,
The Party can never be destroyed.
For it is the vanguard of the masses
And pursues its battle with classic methods,
Which grow from the knowledge of reality.[50]

Holy Order and Elite Corps

In the ideologies the elite is essential as the corps of those initi-

[49] "Das Lied von der Partei," in Ulrich Thomas, *Staatsmacht und Ersatzreligion* ("Sonderausgabe für das Bundesministerium für gesamtdeutsche Fragen"; Munich: Schaefer Verlag, 1961), p. 41.
[50] "Lob der Partei," *ibid.*

ated into the mysteries. The elite communicate, and translate into action, their insights into the determinative ideas. They make the wheels of the movement turn. Even with the widespread appeal during the French Revolution to "the general will" one meets the Babouvist defense of an enlightened vanguard.[51] The lives of the elite are dedicated to the cause to a degree never expected of the masses. Along with dedication goes an austerity of mind and body which far surpasses the capacity of ordinary people. Max Eastman has described the "stern and sublime heritage of martyr-faith" which animated the early revolutionaries in Russia: "They became almost a noble order, a selected stock of men and women who could be relied upon to be heroic, like a Knight of the Round Table or the Samurai, but with the patents of their nobility in the future, not the past."[52] Americans have no valid insights into the rigors of Communist party life—the careful screening, the indoctrination, and the "holy rules" to be obeyed. In his book *Why They Behave Like Russians* John Fischer writes:

> When a young Russian aspires to membership in the Party, he renounces the worldly life and dedicates himself to what the Webbs have called "the vocation of leadership." He puts aside all other faiths, including Christianity, and learns to shun such abstruse heresies as "rotten liberalism" and "rightist deviation." After a long apprenticeship in good works and study of the sacred books, his name is put forward by three old members, and, if his record, character, and knowledge of the Marxian scriptures can pass the examination of the hierarchy, he finally is sworn into the order.[53]

In certain significant respects the elite corps forms the "clerical order" of the political scene. The members are inducted into the theoretical subtleties of the ideology by the most intense and de-

[51] J. L. Talmon, *The Origins of Totalitarian Democracy* (New York: Praeger, 1960), pp. 209-14.

[52] Quoted in Edmund Wilson, *To the Finland Station* (Garden City: Doubleday Anchor Books, 1953), p. 454. Reprinted by permission of Doubleday and Company, Inc.

[53] New York: Harper, 1946, p. 65.

tailed instruction; they are ordained in their function by specific vows, even in specific chapter rooms or sacred places. Hitler trained his political leaders in secular seminaries, the *Ordensburgen.* Here they were taught by "the best teachers in history and science of race, philosophy and culture, economics and specialized training, etc."[54] The *Burgmänner,* the graduates of the *Ordensburgen,* were to become the spiritual and ideological leaders of National Socialism; the Order would insure the doctrinal purity and vitality of the next *Führergeneration.* The *Nazi Primer* was reassuring: "A new nobility, the nobility of accomplishment and work, will guarantee the future of folk and Reich."[55]

The morality of the SS man required that he be ready to sacrifice himself for the sake of an idea. Death for an idea was understood to be life's highest fulfillment.[56] But loyalty to the idea was expressed by way of loyalty to the Führer. Here is the oath taken by the SS man:

I swear loyalty and bravery to you, Adolf Hitler, as *Führer* and Reichs Chancellor. I vow to you, and to those you have named to command me, obedience unto death, so help me God.[57]

As the war years drew on Hitler came to place ever more confidence in this saving remnant. He had expressed his ideal: "I want the German boy to be weatherproof, quick as a greyhound, tough as leather, hard as Krupp steel."[58]

Sacred Icons—Posters and Pictures

Where the hero cannot reveal his physical presence he can be present in facsimile—in statues, portraits, and idealized pictures.

[54] *Nazi Conspiracy and Aggression,* VI, 240.
[55] *Op. cit.,* p. 77.
[56] Cf. "Heldische Morgenfeier NSDAP Ortsgruppe Sparenberg," *Westfalische Neueste Nachrichten,* March 19, 1938.
[57] *Nazi Conspiracy and Aggression,* VI, 134.
[58] Quoted by Emmet Hughes, "Berlin under Siege," *Life,* July 19, 1948, p. 72.

The hero is always portrayed as benign and strong; his likeness reminds the viewer that Big Brother is always solicitous for one's welfare. Portraits of Marx, Lenin, Stalin, and Khrushchev have been ubiquitous in Communist lands.[59] Any interest in realism has had to give way to idealized portrayal: the serenity and profundity of the leader is to attach, through the symbolic process, to the movement itself. The Socialist movement, moreover, has made extensive use of vivid posters to direct attention to social ills; more interest has been shown in the poster's emotive value than in its cognitive function. Caricature and satire have played prominent roles in the propagandistic use of posters.

Of particular interest here, however, is the manner in which the political iconographers have utilized age-old religious and cultural associations in the service of a new allegiance. The symbolism of the great ideologies is rooted in diverse historical traditions and is shaped by older national patterns. This is to be seen particularly with reference to Eastern Orthodoxy. The unique Russian religiousness, so attached to the sacred icons, cannot dispense completely with them. Although the themes contrast sharply with those of the holy images the new icons elicit a religious quality of devotion. As one visitor has observed, in place of the religious medallion or the image of the Virgin one will now find in Moscow tiny badges worn by the new faithful with a portrait of Lenin as a child.[60]

The corner which had been set aside in many Eastern Orthodox homes for the holy icons, with a vigil candle burning constantly before them, has been rededicated to the icons of the secular saviors. In homes, schools, and factories it became the "red corner." On the great holy days, e.g., Epiphany and the Czar's birthday, the well-known icons from the churches were carried

---

[59] Cf., e.g., John Steinbeck's reflection on the statues, busts, paintings, and photographs of Stalin in Russia, in *A Russian Journal* (New York: The Viking Press, 1948), pp. 49-51.

[60] James Morris, "First Visit to a Muffled Colossus," *New York Times Magazine,* July 3, 1960, p. 27.

through the streets in procession. Since the Revolution, new icons have been carried in procession; devotion has been rechanneled. With all recognition of the careful staging, the participation by decree, and the authentic political elements present here, the parades of Communist workers and youth, with their plethora of portraits and color, can be understood adequately only in religious terms. Another devotion animates the participants in these processions, and the devotion acknowledges nothing beyond the new Kingdom of Man.

Shibboleths

Mottoes and slogans are, like the biblical "shibboleth," inevitable instruments for determining and cementing loyalties. When the slogan can be joined in wholeheartedly by the individual it serves to reinforce enthusiasm. The French revolutionary slogan *Liberté, Égalité, Fraternité* was a powerful reinforcement of loyalty to the First Republic, and it has retained much of its original vitality to this day. A slogan can serve to steel resistance and call forth courage. How can one weigh the significance for Poles of the terse phrase *Jesccze Polska nie zingela* ("Poland is Unconquered!")?

A slogan is useful whether facts reinforce the slogan or whether the slogan shrouds unpleasant facts. Few slogans could be more powerful than that following the October Revolution, "Peace, Bread, and Land." The *narodnik* writers had cast the cultured classes under the spell of "the authority of the soil."[61] An unsuccessful war, universal famine, and a feudal order all prepared the Russian peasantry for a new dispensation. Nothing could appeal to the peasant's love for the land and to his longing for a few acres of soil so much as the magical promise of a small estate. On the vast scale of Russian discontent this succinct formula for salvation was as dramatic as the closing words of the *Communist Manifesto,* which one now sees hung above Lenin's bed in the museum

---

[61] Cf. Nicholas Berdyaev, *The Origin of Russian Communism,* trans. R. M. French (Ann Arbor: University of Michigan Press, 1960), pp. 17 and 58 ff.

restoration of his bedroom: "Workers of the World, Unite!"[62] During Easter celebrations today in Moscow the Young Communist League proclaims its slogan "Lenin is with us" to counter the traditional response of believers to the priest's proclamation of Christ's resurrection: "He is risen indeed!"

Today placards and inscriptions are in such evidence in Communist Europe and Asia that man comes to see himself as a creature manipulated by the symbol-wielders. The time comes when stereotyped symbols become devoid of appeal and hollow in identity. At certain points in their speeches orators in the Iron Curtain countries simply stop speaking and begin clapping. They are not applauding themselves but the idea; the action is a ritual reinforcement of the ideology.

National Socialism profited by ambiguity; it succeeded in appropriating to itself the blessed slogans of the Right and Left, of nationalists and socialists.[63] Apprehensive workers and reluctant industrialists became organic parts of the new order through the slogan *Gemeinnutz geht vor Eigennutz* ("The Public Good before Private Good"), and the vast majority of Germans could identify themselves with *Brechung der Zinsknechtschaft* ("Break the Reparations Enslavement") and *Deutschland Erwache* ("Germany, Wake Up!"). The Nazis tried to capitalize on the spiritual concomitants of labor with the slogan *Kraft durch Freude* ("Strength through Joy"). In its slogans the Nazi movement incorporated its central themes: duty, strength, honor, the Führer, comradeship, loyalty, obedience, bravery. In place of the custom in many German churches, stemming from the practice of the Moravian Brethren, of selecting a Bible verse to serve as the saying of the week, the propaganda ministry attempted to promote one of the Führer's sayings as the thought of the week, e.g., *Deutschland ist da, wo starke Herzen sind* ("Germany is found where brave hearts can be found"). They emblazoned a grim gospel above the gates of most

[62] Edmund Wilson, *op. cit.,* p. 474.
[63] Hannah Arendt, *Origins of Totalitarianism,* p. 347.

concentration camps: "Hard Work Will Make You Free." Strangely enough, Walter Ulbricht proclaims this same gospel to the citizens of East Germany.

But it is in the "German greeting" that one meets the full religious significance of what became a universal shibboleth. Romano Guardini has examined the "Heil Hitler" with clarity and precision:

> Of particular importance was a phenomenon which occurred everywhere in daily life, namely, the so-called German greeting. It must become clear immediately to every Catholic Christian that the "Heil Hitler!" was meant as the counterpart to the age-old greeting, "Praised be Jesus Christ." (Hitler himself, as well as his chief of propaganda, Goebbels, were, of course, apostate Catholics.) And what does this mean? What, after all, is the meaning of a greeting? Very ancient feelings are operative here: if I meet someone I can trust, I wish him well by my greeting; if he is a stranger, that is, hostile at first meeting, I must set his strength against someone else. Thus, seen from the standpoint of the history of religions, the greeting is one of the simplest forms of piety: community and meeting, exorcism and parrying. Quite logically the name of the Redeemer, Jesus Christ, appears in it with the Christian re-interpretation of existence. In the place of Jesus' name was placed the name of Hitler. Of course, the greeting was, as a rule, carried out quite thoughtlessly. But in its essential meaning it signified two things. First, one wished well-being *(Heil)* to the man named in it at every meeting, that is, innumerable times in the course of a day. All the strength and good fortune which the well-wishing of these hearts could bring about was to concentrate on him. But the greeting signified something more. Not only was well-being wished upon Hitler. One wished upon the person he met that Hitler's well-being should come upon him, as the counterpart and replacement of what the faithful meant when they wished someone the grace of Jesus Christ.[64]

Sacred Times

It is well known that the festivals of the Christian church stand in obvious and conscious relationship to pagan festivals of Roman

---

[64] *Der Heilbringer,* pp. 42-43.

antiquity and to local observances antedating the beginnings of Christianity. The Christian church adopted and transformed the Roman and Germanic celebrations, it baptized them and employed them in its own economy of salvation. In the modern world the opportunity has been offered anti-Christian thought forms to reverse this action. Auguste Comte, with his catechism and calendar of saints, was the most thoroughgoing. His new humanity celebrated its copious virtues in the festivals of a new year.

Few since Comte have attempted a scheme as inclusive and colorful as his, but Comte's proposals had been anticipated and explored earlier in the Jacobin clubs. The revolutionary faith of the Jacobins had expressed itself in a symbolism clearly borrowed from Roman Catholicism. July 14, Bastille Day, was a "holy festival," a day "when man is resuscitated and born anew in his rights."[65] The societies observed the birth registrations of their initiates, listened to sermons with theological motifs, venerated the martyrs of the revolution, sang patriotic hymns, and honored the Declaration of the Rights of Man.[66] There are consistent parallels here with the Catholic rites against which the Jacobins revolted. The new cult of Reason was to unite France spiritually and politically. Robespierre worked out a complete cult for revolutionary democracy. J. L. Talmon says of Robespierre's new mysticism: "There are no other priests than the magistrates, religious and patriotic ceremonial are the same, and to serve your country is to serve God."[67] Following is the "Text of the Draft of a Writ Presented by Robespierre to the National Convention":

I. The French people recognize the existence of the Supreme Being and the immortality of the soul.

II. They recognize that the worship of the Supreme Being is the practice of man's duties.

---

[65] Labroue, "La Société Populaire de la Garde-Freinet," *Révolution Française,* LIV (1908), 155. Cited by Crane Brinton, "Revolutionary Symbolism in the Jacobin Clubs," *American Historical Review,* XXXII (1926-27), 737-52.

[66] *Ibid.*

[67] J. L. Talmon, *op. cit.,* p. 24.

III.   In the first rank among these duties stands the obligation to hate bad faith and tyranny, to punish tyrants and traitors, to succor the unfortunate, to respect the weak, to defend the oppressed, to do for others all the good one can, and not to be unjust to oneself.

IV.   Festivals shall be instituted to recall men to the thought of the divinity and to the dignity of his being.

V.   They shall borrow their names from the glorious events of our Revolution, from the most cherished virtues and those most useful to mankind, from the noblest benefactions of nature.

VI.   The French Republic shall celebrate each year the festivals of July 14, 1789; August 10, 1792; January 21, 1793; May 31, 1793.

VII.   They shall celebrate in groups of ten days the festivals listed as follows: To the Supreme Being and to Nature; To the Human Race; To the French People; To the Benefactors of Humanity; To the Martyrs of Liberty; To Liberty and to Equality; To the Republic; To the Freedom of the World; To Love of the Native Land; To the Hatred of Tyrants and of Traitors; To Truth; To Justice; To Modesty; To Glory and Immortality; To Friendship; To Frugality; To Courage; To Good Faith; To Heroism; To Disinterestedness; To Stoicism; To Love; To Conjugal Love; To Paternal Love; To Maternal Tenderness; To Filial Piety; To Infancy; To Youth; To Manhood; To Old Age; To Misfortune; To Agriculture; To Industry; To Our Forefathers; To Posterity; To Happiness.

VIII.   The Committees of Public Safety and of Public Instruction are charged with presenting a plan of organization for these festivals.

IX.   The National Convention invites all the talent worthy to serve the cause of humanity to the honor of contributing to the establishment of these festivals through hymns and civic songs and by all the media which can contribute to their embellishment and utility.

X.   The Committee of Public Safety shall distinguish the works which appear to them the most fitting to realize these objectives and shall recompense their authors.

XI.   Freedom of worship is retained, in keeping with the decree of the 18th of *frimaire*.[68]

XII.   Every aristocratic concourse and those contrary to public order will be dispersed.

XIII.   In the case of troubles motivated or caused by any cult whatsoever, those who shall instigate such by their fanatical preaching or by their counter-revolutionary insinuations, and those who

---

[68] *Frimaire* was the third month of the first French republic; *prairial* was the ninth month.

shall provoke them by their unjust and ungrateful violence, shall be punished impartially according to the rigor of the laws.

XIV. A special report shall be made regarding the disposition of detail in connection with the present decree.

XV. There will be celebrated on the 20th of *prairial* next a festival in honor of the Supreme Being.

David is in charge of presenting the plan to the National Convention.[69]

In America our rites of consecration, such as Mother's Day, Memorial Day, the Fourth of July, and Veterans Day, celebrate the moral values of motherhood, self-sacrifice, liberty, and patriotism. The religion of democracy emerges from sermons and speeches and Veterans Day addresses without number. Following is an excerpt from a speech by a leader of the Sons of Union Veterans on Memorial Day:

> We meet to honor those who fought, but in so doing we honor ourselves. From them we learn a lesson of sacrifice and devotion and of accountability to God and honor. We have an inspiration for the future today—our character is strengthened—this day speaks of a better and greater devotion to our country and to all that our flag represents.
>
> Our flag, may we see thee, love thee, and live thee. Our country, may we see thee, love thee, and live thee. Let the flag be an inspiration that our youth may not be subject to pernicious influences. Washington and Betsy Ross created our flag out of a few strips of cloth. May we honor it as the emblem of our country.[70]

Secular holidays function for many as religious holy days, and Christian holy days are also observed as secular holidays. In actual fact, the panoply of American holidays bears a striking resemblance to Robespierre's "Writ," though the fervor of revolutionary resentment is lacking. Moreover, one misses the totalitarian leveling of the planes of existence to the single, political plane. Poli-

---

[69] Cited by A. Aulard, *Le Culte de la Raison et Le Culte de L'Être Suprême* (Paris: Felix Alcan, 1909), pp. 273-75.

[70] Quoted by W. Lloyd Warner, *op. cit.,* p. 267.

tics does not emerge as the sole sphere of thought and action, though there are many hints that a consistent view would lead to this conclusion.

Fascism and Nazism, like revolutionary democracy, attempted to break with the reckoning of time from the birth of Christ: time was to be reckoned from the beginnings of the Fascist and the Nazi eras. These eras were ushered in by spectacular acts of spiritual and military power. For example, the Fascist march on Rome on October 28, 1922, had all the overtones of triumphal entry on the part of ancient Roman generals. Nazi publicity attempted to redirect the religious sentiments and convictions surrounding the Christian year. It attempted to celebrate a new religious consciousness which was then arising creatively from the German folk. Old meanings of festivals were suppressed and new meanings were devised. The Christmas celebration, for example, has been most significant in German homes; it centers about Christ's crib, the mother and child, the shepherds, and the familiar Christmas cards. But in the Nazi celebration it centered upon the battle between light and darkness and on the Christmas season as a time of renewal.[71] Easter was reinterpreted in a similar fashion, in the celebrations of the Hitler Youth, as the victory of life over death and the symbol of the resurrection of the German people. March 16, the day on which general conscription was resumed in 1935, was celebrated as Hero's Memorial Day. Other German holidays were dedicated to the German family, the Hitler Youth, the Party Day, and many other causes. November 9 was a variety of All Saints Day in the Third Reich: the fourteen earliest martyrs had fallen before the Feldherrnhalle in Munich in 1923, "in loyal faith in the reawakening of their people."[72] Here is the extravagant proposal, from

[71] Cf. "Soldatenblätter und Weihnachtsfest—ein Briefwechsel," *Vierteljahreshefte für Zeitgeschichte,* I, 3 (1953), 297-99.

[72] Inscription on the commemorative marker in Munich. Cf. *Das Bauen im Dritten Reich,* published in collaboration with Gerdy Troost (3rd, enlarged ed.; Bayreuth: Gauverlag Bayerische Ostmark, 1941), p. 47.

the Reich's Propaganda Office for the Planning and Execution of National Socialist Festivals, for the festive form to honor these men:

> What is envisaged is a very specific *rite,* according to which in the future every festive hour should be structured within the framework of a public *state cult.* It is only on the path of the observance of a definitely structured plan that we shall find gradually emerging, in the course of development, *festive forms* of a liturgical character, the validity of which will last for centuries. To the fixed form of the National Socialist hours of consecration belongs, among other things, the *proclamation* which stands at the center (festive words, 15-20 minute festive addresses, verses of poetry). Following this is the *confession,* spoken by the choir. Connected with this is the *song of dedication* (accompanied and sung in unison, if possible, by all formations). Further, the *invocation of the Führer* (the "Sieg Heil" with the Deutschland Song and the Horst Wessel Song, a verse of each).

From the proclamation of the ninth of November the following sentences are particularly significant:

> At these steps of the Feldherrnhalle, to which today high pilgrimage is made, there once arose a sacrament of battle. And only those belong to its sole cathedral, which is today called Germany, who hammer deep into their own deeds the spirit which motivated these men. Pilgrims you are if you bear the glory of the people higher than the revelations of all religions.

> > You sense the holiness of the Feldherrnhalle.
> > What now the worth of litanies, of prayers at Mass,
> > The polished incense vessels brandished heav'nwards,
> > When matched against the dull rhythm of our drums,
> > When our Führer marches to the steps—?
> > The breath of those who see him snuffs out
> >   the light of the earth,
> > Which, trembling at the advance, is now still.
> > The noise cowers grayly at this, the end of the world:
> >
> > THE FÜHRER RISES!
> >
> > The Führer lifts his hand in the eternal greeting.
> > He strikes his breast in the breast-beat of his
> >   people.

90

. . . .
The Führer's stride today is prayer . . .
He rises and stands, surrounded all by wonder.
He burns with the faith of his comrades.
And no priestly consecration ascends more mightily
Than this mute, stone-structured prayer of the man
In whose nature a people moves.
The Feldherrnhalle oath is our petition to our
    creator,
If only the banner, our banner, stands!
Then it towers aloft: the German high altar!
And before it the standards exult:
What is death when you require our life,
                 GERMANY![73]

But events in the tragic history of Germany have elicited new martyrs and new martyrs' and confessors' days. Each decade calls forth martyrs to protest the old order. The new saints of the forties became those who offered their lives on the glorious twentieth of July in the attempt to assassinate Hitler. And the new saints of the fifties were the strikers of the East Zone who arose as the underprivileged class in the German "workers' paradise."

Given the conflict between Christian doctrine and Communist ideology certain calendar revisions become inevitable also for Communism. Thus in the heyday of Stalin's power parades in his honor celebrated his birthday, the festive holiday spirit of Christmastide was reinterpreted to center on the secular deliverer's birth on December 21, and references to the Christ child were replaced or banned. The Christmas tree was replaced by the "winter tree," and in place of old Saint Nicholas or Santa Claus children received their gifts from the Soviet "Father Frost."

Whitsunday, or Pentecost, stands as one of the great feast days in the Christian church year. Traditionally it is celebrated in European lands with dancing, bunting, and greenery. In the last decade it has become the day for mass rallies of workers' and

[73] These excerpts are taken from a letter circulated within the party by the Propaganda Office; reproduced in Karl Immer, *op. cit.,* pp. 23-24.

youth organizations, when hundreds of thousands of enthusiastic young people have demonstrated for peace and unity.

May 1 has enjoyed a history checkered with belligerent demonstrations of enraged workers and orderly trade-union rallies, with strikes and proclamations, with violence and special pleas. Communists and National Socialists have each called the day their own. Like the May Day rites of the Middle Ages, the day hails the opening of a new era of social progress. In 1889 the first congress of the "Second Socialist International," meeting in Paris, proclaimed May 1 the day of a "large international manifestation for the eight-hour working day." Soon the manifestation of "proletarian class consciousness" began to overshadow the demand for shorter working hours. Nazism endeavored to reinterpret the festival as a symbol of German unity standing in contrast with the disorderly demonstrations of Communist hordes. More recently the day has come to mean little more than a "day off" or a "holiday in honor of the worker" for West Germans, whereas in the Soviet Zone it has been marked by massive demonstrations of armed "workers' fighting groups" parading with units of the Peoples' Police and the Peoples' Army.[74]

Another holiday which constitutes a holy day for a sixth of the earth's surface making up the U.S.S.R. is November 7. It was on this day that the Soviet government was established following the October Revolution. Soviet calendar revision causes the anniversary to fall in November, thirteen days later, but the occasion stands out as a symbol of freedom and progress.

There are, in addition, many days which enjoy secondary or ill-defined levels of authority, with wide variations to be noted in their "sacred" character and observance. Lenin Day (April 22), Karl Marx Day (May 5), Friedrich Engels Day (November 28), the Day of Peace (September 1) are prominent in the new calendar. Greeting cards are available in East German stores for some of these special days, as, for example, Youth Dedication, Name

[74] Cf. The Bulletin (Bonn: Presse- und Informationsamt der Bundesregierung), V, 17 (May 2, 1957), 5, and VI, 16 (April 29, 1958), 4-5.

Giving, the Day of the Peoples' Army, Teachers' Day, Railroaders' Day, Miners' Day, and Freedom Day. Stores are reluctant to carry such items, however, since there are few requests for them.[75] But as years pass one may anticipate that the position of these days will become more firmly entrenched and their ritual usage will be regularized.

Visual Symbols

As hopes have attached to new messages these hopes have been symbolized and visualized by new symbols of power and victory: in the place of the cross we meet the invincible swastika, or the memorable fasces, or the purposeful hammer and sickle. These visual symbols have the power of clustering about themselves rich overtones of meaning and association.

The banners which played such a prominent role in Nazi ritual were very similar to the banners carried in Southern German religious processions.[76] In Nazi circles they became the symbol of spiritual communion. Around them and for them the formations fought: they were never to be lost and, if need be, one was to die for them. At the festive consecration of new banners a German pastor could say of them:

> The banner is the bond of fellowship, of loyalty. It is the silent exhortation to fulfillment of duty and of service. It speaks a quiet language of obedience and discipline.
>
> The swastika, this glorious symbol, demonstrates to the world that in Germany today a strong faith prevails in a single Reich, in a proud, united people.[77]

Hannah Arendt points to the similarity between sacred societies and the totalitarian movements, particularly in the area of ritual. She writes:

[75] "Namensweihe in Dresden," *Frankfurter Allgemeine Zeitung,* July 20, 1959.
[76] Editorial note in the Reynal and Hitchcock edition of *Mein Kampf* (New York, 1939), p. 507.
[77] "Fahnenweihe in der Christuskirche," *Beilage der Niedersächsischen Tageszeitung,* October 11, 1933.

The marches around the Red Square in Moscow are in this respect no less characteristic than the pompous formalities of the Nuremberg party days. In the center of the Nazi ritual was the so-called "blood banner," and in the center of the Bolshevik ritual stands the mummified corpse of Lenin, both of which introduce a strong element of idolatry into the ceremony.[78]

In nothing is the strength of symbols so apparent as when a symbol which is a mark of glory becomes a means of humiliation: in Hitler's law requiring Jews to display prominently a yellow, six-pointed star, or when the opponents of Nazism set the swastika in direct conflict with the star of David, or when opponents shatter the symbols of a group, overturn the statues of dictators—Sulla and Pompey, Stalin and Peron—attack churches, deface icons, desecrate altars, and burn flags, and thereby symbolically annihilate the group. The storming of the Bastille and of the Winter Palace were greater as symbolic victories than as military turning-points. Attacks on the old order are always first directed against its symbols; the "false" values of a regime are communicated through "false" symbols, symbols which participate in charlatanry and deception. Where symbols are used destroyers of symbols will always arise, men who in the name of truth will cry out against the magical associations of images and the hollow repetition of formulas.

One of the most effective symbols in Communist propaganda has been the "peace dove"; whether in art or in real life, the symbol allows for infinite varieties of pleasant associations. Yet even such a symbol could be turned against itself by the non-partisan periodical *Paix et Liberté* when it designed quite another dove, "the dove that goes boom."

Sacred Scriptures

Attention has often been drawn to the sacred scriptures of the ideologies. The "canon" of a movement is usually not closed and

[78] *The Origins of Totalitarianism*, p. 365.

adherents are scarcely aware of the "sacred" character of their authorities. Documents vary in the degree of approval accorded them and in the function they are intended to fulfill: one may point to catechisms, for example, the *Catechism of a Revolutionist* from the French revolution, and sacred writings, such as *Mein Kampf, The Communist Manifesto,* and *Das Kapital.* Jules Michelet was one of the earliest to provide a new sacred scripture in *La Bible de l'humanité* of 1864.

The character of the volumes conforms to that of each movement, *Das Kapital* with its scientific pretensions, *Mein Kampf* with its glorification of force. Nowhere, perhaps, does the sacred character of *Mein Kampf* emerge more dramatically than in the plan for the National Reich Church. The volume was declared to be "the greatest of all documents," the "most sacred future book"; editions were to conform exactly in content and pagination to the popular edition; it alone was to be placed on the altar, and it was to be expounded to the congregation as the text for National Church speakers.[79] Such a view could easily be taken of the inventions of political wizardry when the Holy Scriptures of Christianity were understood as a set of moral laws or as a symbol of man's quest for truth.

Confession and Penance

Confessions and purgings were a distinct feature of the Jacobin clubs;[80] their ideology made orthodoxy imperative and deviation heretical. However, the question of orthodox and unorthodox is relevant for each of the ideologies, though wide ranges of difference prevail regarding latitude of opinion. Communism has faced

[79] Cf. Stewart Herman, *It's Your Souls We Want* (New York: Harper and Brothers, 1943), Appendix I, pp. 298-99. (The appendix contains the text of the "30-Point Church Plan.") Oskar Söhngen, *Säkularisierter Kultus* (Gütersloh: Bertelsmann, 1950), p. 55, points to another volume which became a kind of "substitute Bible" for the movement. It was the "German Housebook" which was published in enormous editions by the Central Office on Cultural Affairs for distribution to German families.

[80] Cf. Crane Brinton, *op. cit.,* pp. 745-46.

the question in an infinite variety of forms—Proudhonism and Bakuninism, Stalinism and Trotskyism, Marxism and Leninism, revisionism and gradualism, revolutionary upheaval and peaceful coexistence. Berdyaev has described the line from one faith to another in the Soviet Union:

> The religious energy of the Russian spirit possesses the faculty of switching over and directing itself to purposes which are not merely religious, for example, to social objects. In virtue of their religious-dogmatic quality of spirit, Russians—whether orthodox, heretics or schismatics—are always apocalyptic or nihilist. . . . And there always remains as the chief thing the profession of some orthodox faith; this is always the criterion by which membership of the Russian people is judged.[81]

The Communist conception of the body politic, in particular, requires a single and unified point of view. This is bound up with the traditional conception of *sobornost,* or congregationalism, according to which truth resides, not in individuals, but in the brotherhood. The Russian conception of the organic society is related to this religious concept: the individual is bound to the Christian community of love in an organic relationship; salvation is a collective rather than a distinctly individual phenomenon; each individual is closely related to others, in terms of absolute goals and values, by a unity of belief.[82] A crime against the brotherhood must be confessed and it must be expiated; there is a vital sense of the dialectic of guilt and forgiveness, condemnation and acquittal active here. But there have been innumerable prisoners in Moscow's horrid Lubianka and in Berlin's dark Hohenschönhausen who have had no charges placed against them. They were considered dangerous elements because they would not agree with the orthodox theory.

Such confessions have not been absent from American soil.

---

[81] Nicholas Berdyaev, *op. cit.,* p. 9. Used by permission of the publishers, Goeffrey Bles and The University of Michigan Press.

[82] Cf. Ernst Benz, *The Eastern Orthodox Church,* pp. 157 ff.

Richard Wright, the late Negro writer, tells of the trial of a Communist comrade on Chicago's South side. First, an absolute was established, a definitive picture of global struggle. Then, slowly, a new sense of reality, a conception of shared life on earth, was enthroned in the intimate comradeship. Finally, the accused voluntarily sobbed forth his guilt, for he had been given "new eyes" through which to view his crime.[83]

According to another traditional concept, that of kenoticism, the imitation of Christ in his voluntary death for mankind, one is to be ready by his self-sacrifice to merge with the mass of the people. Sir John Maynard traces the transition in his *Russia in Flux:*

> The echoes of religious thought in the brain of anti-religious Communists ring yet further, if more faintly, in that strange passion for confession and self-humiliation which the trials of the Communists fallen into disfavour have revealed to a puzzled world. . . . What excommunication is to the pious Catholic, that, to the Orthodox, is separation from the congregation of the brethren, in which truth and love alike reside. He must seek restoration by the abjuration of all errors and the confession of all sins. *Outside of the congregation he cannot be right.*
>
> The religious conception of the presence of truth in the congregation passed to the Communists. . . . But the majority is on the side of the Government: and the offender, alone more than all, in the humiliation of his soul.[84]

To be sure, men like Tito and Kardelj have been able to make significant and threatening breaks with uniform theory, but the Soviet center has been able to maintain the primacy and authority of its own interpretation at home, in Western Europe, and in Communist missionary lands.

The interest in ideological conformity has frequently been so

---

[83] *The God that Failed,* ed. by Richard Crossman (New York: Bantam Books, 1952), pp. 156 ff.

[84] John Maynard, *Russia in Flux* (New York: Macmillan, 1948), pp. 441-42. Copyright 1941 and 1942 by The Macmillan Company, New York; reprinted by permission of the publisher.

strong that the disinterestedness of scientific research has been affected: "capitalist" or "idealist" science must either give way before the scientific objectivity of dialectical materialism, or it must follow previous Soviet accomplishments. The diversity of conflicting opinion in "imperialist" countries is a sign of their lack of direction and weakness. The "discussion groups," brain washing, and confessions through which hundreds of thousands have passed in Communist lands are designed to crush resistance and to achieve a unified point of view. The regret shown there for deviations can properly and revealingly be compared with Christian penitence; and it has been religious leaders, whether Protestant or Catholic, who have formed the most disturbing centers of resistance in Communist countries.

Although confessions were already employed by the Russians in the trials of the thirties, brain washing and confessional techniques have been utilized most extensively by the Chinese Communists, who have not wished to employ the blood baths and slave labor of the Russians.[85] Not only Christianity but the ancient moral philosophies have had to be destroyed. Physical and mental resources for resistance have first been undermined. Then faults, either real or imaginary, have been confessed. Minds have then been reshaped; convictions have been altered and new memories have been installed to replace expunged events. Not only have men's minds been washed, but plays, films, books have been "cleansed" of incorrect or burdensome thoughts. Christian missionaries expelled from China have reported amazement at the similarity between Communist methods and practices and those of the Christian churches. The catechumenate system has been employed in order to teach Communist doctrine.[86] The self-criticism staged before a taunting, appreciative crowd becomes a sort of "common confession"—in contrast with the "private confession" which results from the criticism entered in an appropriate book in one's factory or

[85] Cf. Appendix 4, "Self-Criticism and Confession in Communist China."
[86] Cf. Father Robert Greene, *Calvary in China* (London: Burns Oates, 1954), *passim*.

98

place of work. Here, as in the concentration camps, the plasticity of human nature becomes the determining point: men are to be remade to become useful in the new society.

5

THE NEW RITES OF PASSAGE

> THE *hymn to the Eternal is sung by the people*
> *every morning in the temples; all the public festi-*
> *vals begin with it.*
>
> SAINT-JUST, *Institutions Républicaines* (1794)

It was Friedrich Nietzsche who once observed that European thought has tended to stress the Apollonian, the rational element in life, at the expense of the Dionysian, the sub-rational or emotional.[1] He drew upon Schopenhauer and Wagner in pointing to the whole turgid flow of life as it really is, expressed in the natural, ideal soil of tragic myth, and he contrasted with this the sickness of modern, abstract culture devoid of myth.[2]

The Nazis agreed enthusiastically: they had seen too much barren intellectualism in German philosophy and literature. In the effort to resolve life's problems scientifically they detected a subtle conspiracy against truth. In their new rites and mythologies they descended to the deep, hidden wells of being. They disclaimed the knowledge-craving Socratism of their day and dipped again into Dionysiac ecstasy: they reveled in the night; they bestowed their devotion on sacred, unknown powers, on German soil, on race, blood, and honor. Reason, symbolized in its extremes by Communist theoreticians, they detested as the crassest stupidity. They warned against an over-emphasis on the function of verbal symbols in their life-festivals.[3] Rite, or symbolic action, was seen as historically and ideologically prior to verbal constructs. They snatched their zealots from the perennial conflict to which Nietzsche

---

[1] *The Birth of Tragedy or Hellenism and Pessimism,* trans. William A. Haussmann (Edinburgh: T. N. Foulis, 1909), *passim.*

[2] *Ibid.,* p. 174.

[3] Cf. *Die Gestaltung der Lebensfeiern,* p. 12.

had pointed them and set them on the road to the celebration of the beauty of life in all of its secret horror.

So the National Socialist movement embraced a new doctrine of man and of nature in contrast to the previous development. The Nazi symbols were uniquely effective in appeal, as one may see in their utilization of color, insignia, and martial music. The ornate Nazi ritual provided an avenue for emotional participation. The ritual and dramatic use of light and fire, reminiscent of certain primitive ceremonies, and the emphasis on "living green" in decoration indicate the power of a vitalistic philosophy of nature among the Nazis. These elements of nature were seen as possessing an intrinsic power of life, quite apart from any transcendent source or referent. They were, indeed, related to a history of salvation, the saving history of the German people, but this saving history was deliberately cut off from any transcendent power, or from the biblical events of God's saving activity. There were still frequent references to the "blessings of Providence," to "fate," and to "German destiny," but no one seriously believed any longer in the existence of a personal, self-sufficient, and self-knowing Being. Each authentic re-enactment of the Wagnerian operas, the *Ring* cycle and *Tristan and Isolde,* had the character of a religious service; it was an expression of the vital spirit and will of the German *Volk.* But there were also counterparts to the worship of the Christian church. The structure of the Evangelical service is evident in this "Morning Celebration and Worship Service," printed here with comments (in brackets) by Oskar Söhngen:

Theme: "Where the German Stands One Finds Loyalty"

Fanfare of the Hitler Youth
Entrance March of the Banners
1. Joint Song: "Nothing Can Defraud Us" (H. Spitta)
2. Saying of the Führer:
   Speaker: "The Führer says:
         'Whoever breaks with loyalty

Is lost and must be overthrown!
But one who to his people will loyal be
Will himself by loyalty be known.' "

{The "liturgical" relationship of this maxim to the Introit of Christian worship is quite apparent.}

3. Choir of Hitler Youth: "And if We Hold to Loyalty"
   (Hans Baumann)

4. Honoring of the Dead:
   The Officiant says:
   "Everything great in the world has come into being through loyalty. . . . We honor the dead and lower the banners in their memory."

Joint Song: "The Heavens Gray and the Earth So Brown"
(Altendorf)

{The "Kyrie" part of the Service}

5. Speakers read two examples of representative loyalty:
   a) of a mother who at the beginning of the Second World War gladly offers, in the hour of need, a handful of poor coins, the sole remembrance of her son who fell in World War I
   b) of the mothers from Tirschtiegel who went out to bring home their dead, who had been killed by the Poles, in order to lay them to rest in their native soil.

{The parallel to the lessons in the Christian service}

6. Choir of Hitler Youth: "Where We Stand One Finds Loyalty"

{The "Credo"}

7. Two poems: "The Company" and "My Comrade," recited by two speakers

8. Choir of Hitler Youth: "Attention, Comrade"
   (Hans Baumann)

9 Address: "Loyalty to One's Last Breath"

10. Avowal: "Loyalty can never die;
              As the days run on
              It awakens in one's brethren,
              Who have fallen now. . . ."

{The parallel to the Sermon and the Sermon Hymn}

11. Joint Song: "Earth Creates Anew" (H. Spitta)

Fanfare or Roll of Drums of the Hitler Youth
Exit March of the Banners[4]

The National Socialist "Life Festivals"

An entire series of ceremonies which van Gennep terms, in reference primarily to primitive religions, "rites of passage" were developed under the Nazis and have been refurbished by the Communists. These began with the Birth Festival or Name Giving, the counterpart of Christian baptism. Here are the directions for the National Socialist Birth Festival:

> Along with the legal action of notification and registration at the Registrar's Office, a child's entry into the life of the circle of kinship and acquaintance is marked by a special celebration. The celebration bears the name of *Birth Festival.*
>
> The designation "German," "extra-ecclesiastical," or even "brown" baptism is to be avoided, as is also "Name Dedication." Just as in the case of the actual name giving, the "sponsors' celebration" or "sponsors' pledge" represents only a part of the Birth Festival.
>
> A "Reception into the Peoples' Community" is nonsense. A child born to German parents belongs to the German people's community by virtue of its birth.
>
> The father need not, as in previous generations, acknowledge the child as fit for life, or even "accept" it or incorporate it into the kindred. Today, through National Socialist population politics, we diminish the possibility that unfit children will be born, but, in addition, we are in a position, through medical science, to make able men from premature infants and weak children.
>
> The Birth Festival is neither combat action nor national holiday, but a kin and family festival.
>
> The Birth Festival consists of a number of actions, specifically:
>> Greeting of the Child
>> Name Giving
>> Sponsors' Pledge
>> Honoring the Mother
>> Distribution of Presents (birthday gifts)

[4] From *Die Neue Gemeinschaft,* XI (1942), 607. Reprinted, with comments, in Oskar Söhngen, *Säkularisierter Kultus,* pp. 16-17.

A traditional symbol for birth that is still usable today is the life rune (man rune): Y

Corresponding to the character of the Birth Festival as a family festival is the opportunity that should be given the relatives and close friends of the parents to see the child and bring presents at the Birth Festival. However, excesses are to be avoided in this connection, as, for example, the first greeting of the child with the German greeting.

The law prescribes that notification be made of the birth of each child within seven days at the Registrar's Office.

This notification is an arrangement prescribed by law. It should normally be done by the father himself. The birth will be announced from the Registrar's Office. The first name of the child, however, can be reported as late as one month after the birth.

In order to cull out non-German first names, and particularly Jewish and ecclesiastical first names, the NSDAP [the Nazi Party] and its organizations, as well as the registrars, will advise all Party members and people's colleagues regarding the choice of first names. For this purpose a register of German names will be made available. After its appearance the point must be reached where a Birth Festival is conducted as a Life Festival of the Movement only if the child is given a German name.

On the basis of the National Socialist world-view special emphasis must be placed on the presence of the mother, too, at the Birth Festival. For that reason the celebration normally takes place after her recovery.

On the other hand, the celebration should not be postponed so long that the birth of the child is no longer experienced as an event, that the child has already grown away from the narrow sphere of the mother, or that the name has already become a self-evident matter.

The Birth Festival as a "Life Festival of the Movement" takes place, with the participation of the Party, primarily within the family and the kindred. To these are added the sponsors and, in some instances, a circle of friends and companions. In no case is it to be conducted as a public event. Mass celebrations, at which the births of many children are celebrated at the same time and in the same room, are to be avoided.

It is desirable that for each child several sponsors (*Bürgen, Gevatter, Göde*—the terminology varying according to local custom) be chosen from the relationship or circle of friends or acquaintances (e.g., a blood relative and a companion). If possible, men and women from the parents' own generation should be chosen as sponsors. The number of sponsors differs according to locality. It is desirable to ask at least one man and one woman to serve as sponsors for a child.

In the National Socialist people's community the role of sponsor is to carry with it a deep sense of obligation. It must not be an empty form. People who are to be associated with the parents as sponsors should be such as can and will help the child if the parents should be involved in any kind of tragedy.

The NSDAP must emphasize the fact that this intervention on behalf of another person with respect to the National Socialist world-view becomes a fixed and binding obligation.

The above is of particular importance in the case of children born out of wedlock.

The sponsors do not, in fact, always belong to the kindred by reason of blood; but on the basis of their obligation they belong ideationally. Therefore they have a part in all the events within the kindred, particularly when these involve the child they sponsored.

It is desirable that the sponsor be named guardian by the parents *(Par. 1776, Absatz I, Ziffer 1 und 2, BGB)* and that the Court of Ward appoint the sponsor as a guardian *(Par. 1779, Absatz I, BGB)*.

The Birth Festival should be primarily a family celebration. At its center stands the act of honoring by the ranking official (block leader) or by his delegate. In connection with this he hands out the artistically arranged birth certificate (from the Registrar's Office) and the commemorative sheet with the Führer's statement. The father carries out the Name Giving.

The sponsors obligate themselves by shaking hands with the parents.

It is meaningless to address the child at length in a speech, since the child doesn't understand the words anyway.

If a Birth Festival as a Life Festival of the Movement does not take place, then the ranking official (block leader) or his delegate conveys to the family the good wishes of the Party and the commemorative sheet.*

Already before the birth of the child the ranking official (per-

---

* In Gau Steiermark, for example, a Birth Festival was conducted at the Registrar's Office, by request, for all those people's comrades for whom there was no Birth Festival as Life Festival of the Movement.

haps with the aid of the NS-Frauenschaft and the NSV [auxiliary organizations of the party]) will determine, or have determined, the parents' wishes with regard to the choice of a name and arrangements for the celebration.

The foregoing regulations apply also in the case of children born out of wedlock.[5]

The Birth Festival was followed by the *Verpflichtungsfeier,* or "Festival of Obligation." This served the same purpose under Nazism which the Youth Dedication serves today under Communism. It was the counterpart of the rite of confirmation. But under Nazism it served as a puberty rite, the occasion for a personal decision and a solemn confession to folk and Führer. The young person vowed to live as a German youth, ready at all times and places to bear the Führer's name and faithfully to serve his leader and the German people.[6]

There were also appropriate forms for marriage and burial. These crucial events in the cycle of life, which early man experienced as mysterious and awesome, still carry a religious significance, and in the rites of the ideologies they still reflect the power of being. It was a natural and inevitable development that Nazism should celebrate the key events in the life of the individual and the family. It was held that one became a National Socialist at birth, that the rights of the state began already at this point. The Birth Festival celebrated the gift of life to the newborn infant within the framework of kindred and people. In this, as in other ceremonies, light, or the lighting of candles, became the symbol of the transmission of life from generation to generation. Yet these festivals were not understood to be "cultic" by the Nazis. Christian cult was viewed as world denying. Nazi "custom" was world affirming. Through "custom" the Nazi fulfilled his life in the larger community of his people.[7]

[5] *Die Gestaltung der Lebensfeiern,* pp. 15-18.
[6] Cf. H. Strobel, "Die Verpflichtungsfeier," *Idee und Tat,* 2. Folge (1944). Reprinted in Oskar Söhngen, *op. cit.,* pp. 66-70.
[7] Cf. Appendix 5, "Cult or Custom?"

The marriage ceremony celebrated the progressive extension of family and kindred in the continuing life of the people, since the family was viewed as the original cell of the people. Marriage itself was a holy act in the people's community. Finally, the Festival of the Dead celebrated the return of heroic life to the eternity of the German people. It is significant to note that these festivals were understood not as consecrating or dedicating these events but as bringing the participants to a conscious awareness of the inherent holiness of marriage, birth, and death.[8] They were purveyed as the "visible images" of the National Socialist ideology. They were to "become customs" of the German people.[9]

However, such ceremonies are by no means new. For more than a century the free thinkers in Germany have been promoting their youth dedication ceremony as a counterpart to Roman Catholic first communion and Protestant confirmation. This "third force" continues to sponsor its *Jugendweihe* ("Youth Dedication") in both East and West Germany, but only in East Germany—or "Middle" Germany—is the rite promoted as a state institution. Only here does it reach beyond narrow circles of materialists and free thinkers to become a solemn communal celebration. A similar civic oath was rendered obligatory in the early days of the French Republic. The citizen swore "respect and submission without reservation." He would undertake to "uphold the decrees of the Assembly, even at the peril of life," to "maintain the rights of man and of the citizen," to "live free, or die."[10] A civic cult was already well developed. The following "Official Report of the Civic Baptism Celebrated at Strasbourg, June 13, 1790" asserts that there was no counterpart for such a "democratic" baptism:

The religious altar was elevated. The godmothers carrying the in-

---

[8] Cf. *Die Feier,* p. 14.

[9] Cf. Appendix 6, "Basic Considerations for the National Socialist Life Festivals."

[10] Oath of the Breton Federation of Pontivy, January 15, 1790. Cited in Albert Mathiez, *Les Origines des Cultes Révolutionnaires* (Paris: Société Nouvelle, 1904), pp. 25-26.

fants came to take their places. The flag of the Federation was un-
furled above their heads. The other flags surrounded them, care having been taken, however, not to hide them from the view of the
army and the people. The chiefs and commandants in particular
drew near to serve as witnesses. Then the godfathers, standing
about the altar of the native land, pronounced loudly and distinctly
in the name of their goddaughters, the solemn oath to be faithful to
the nation, to the law, to the king, and to uphold with all their
strength the Constitution enacted by the National Assembly and accepted by the king. The repeated cries "Vive la Nation, Vive la Loi,
Vive le Roi" were sent up immediately from all sides. During these
acclamations the commandants and other chiefs drew their swords
and formed a canopy of steel above the heads of the infants. All the
flags brought together above this canopy appeared in the form of a
dome, with the flag of the Federation surmounting all of them and
seeming to crown the entire arrangement. The swords, grazing together lightly, caused an impressive click to resound, during which
the senior commandant of the confederates fastened a cockade to
each of the infants while pronouncing the words: "My child, I receive you into the national guard. Be a brave and good citizen like
your godfather." It was then that the godmothers offered the children to the native land and held them up for a few moments to the
view of the people. At this point the acclamations redoubled. It left
a feeling in one's soul which cannot be described. Thus there came
to a close a ceremony for which history provides no counterpart.[11]

Name Giving in East Germany

A long tradition, extending from the civic religion of Rousseau
to the Nazi cult of life and fire, stands behind the agitation for
the Youth Dedication in East Germany today.[12] But the Youth
Dedication is only the most crucial and spectacular of many claims
made on the child's loyalty. In school there will be pressures exerted on him to follow the banners of the *Junge Pioniere* ("Young

---

[11] The non-confessional character of this rite is significant: the two daughters,
the one of Lutheran and the other of Roman Catholic parents, had immediately
prior to this been baptized into their own faith. Each had received appropriate
names. The canopy of swords was a feature borrowed from Freemasonry. Cited
in Albert Mathiez, *op. cit.*, p. 44.

[12] Cf. Appendix 7, "Rousseau on Civil Religion."

Pioneers") and the *Freie Deutsche Jugend* ("Free German Youth"). Here, for example, is the Pioneer Youth oath as sworn in the Soviet Union:

> I (a young Pioneer of the Soviet Union)—solemnly swear (before my comrades)—to love my Soviet fatherland ardently—to live, to study, and to fight as the great Lenin willed—and as the Communist Party teaches.[13]

If a student attends a university in East Germany, a declaration of loyalty will be expected of him, such as the following:

> I promise to pursue my studies at the Karl Marx University of Leipzig in the light of socialism, actively to support the policies of the government of the DDR, and on the basis of dialectical and historical materialism to gain a comprehensive education for myself. . . .[14]

Through the bludgeons of report cards, grants, and recommendations, the "religion" of Socialism continues to exact its loyalties. Repeatedly, the simple comment that the Christian answer is "unscientific" or that it "represents a Christian mythology" is used to humiliate and repress. The schools are operated on a Marxist basis and nothing short of a confession of Marxism will satisfy.[15] Again and again the individual will be called upon to annul church membership, since he will be told:

> Resignation from the church is the first step and the beginning of a systematic transmission of our world-view; otherwise we remain standing at the beginning.[16]

[13] From the script of "Meet Comrade Student," presented by the American Broadcasting Co., September, 1962.

[14] *Background Information for Church and Society* (Geneva: World Council of Churches), March, 1959.

[15] Cf. *Kirchliches Jahrbuch* (1960), Anlage 8, "Schreiber von Landesbischof D. Mitzenheim an Staatssekretär Eggerath vom 16.3.1960," p. 164.

[16] *Fahrt Frei* ("Die Wochenzeitung der deutschen Eisenbahner"), No. 26 (East Berlin; July 1, 1958).

In recent years such propaganda has increased sharply. Bishop Otto Dibelius reported at the Synod of East and West Germany in Berlin in April, 1958:

> For Party functionaries, to leave the Church is compulsory. Regular Party members and candidates for Party membership are urged to do the same. Frequent meetings are being held at which the Civic Registrar is ready to issue certificates for those canceling Church affiliation. For officers of the Armed Forces, to leave the Church is compulsory again. Other ranks are urged to do the same.[17]

By means of these new rites and loyalties an altogether new atmosphere, completely purged of Christian associations, is being developed. In the sphere of daily work the individual's private life is merged ever more fully into Socialist collectives, the factories and farms, according to the maxim, "Work Socialistically—Learn Socialistically—Live Socialistically."[18] In their Joint Pastoral Letter of February 8, 1959, the bishops and the Episcopal Commission of the German Democratic Republic summed up the struggle:

> The church is to be replaced. They know what the church and its divine service, its sacraments and its traditions, mean for Christian people. By consecration rites and vows men are to be brought to forget about God and the church and to give themselves solely to this earth, to work, and to society.[19]

In some reports on Communist Name Giving there is frank recognition that it is understood to be an atheistic gesture, in ac-

---

[17] Otto Dibelius, *Report to the Evangelical Church in Germany* (multilithed by the National Lutheran Council, New York; n.d.), p. 3. To indicate the success of this agitation we may note the figures quoted by a West Berlin source for the Evangelical Parish of Halle. During each of the past two years more than 5,000 people declared their abandonment of church connections. Cf. "Churches in Grave Trouble," *Manchester Guardian Weekly*, August 4, 1960, p. 7.

[18] "Die Lage der Kirchen in der Sowjetzone," Part b., *Bulletin* (Bonn: Press- und Informationsamt der Bundesregierung), No. 142 (August 3, 1960), p. 1413.

[19] *Ibid.*, p. 1416.

cordance with "the most recent knowledge of the sciences."[20] Children are called "little citizens of earth."[21] The assertion is regularly made that the ceremony is offered in answer to the requests of many parents. But the promotion through state apparatus and organizations is hardly veiled. Here, for example, are the admonitions of the Mayor of Suhl, in Thuringia, in 1958:

> The citizens of the Suhl district will, with justification, raise the question of why this Name Giving is conducted and who may take part in it. Daily and hourly there occur in the consciousness of our people changes which are based on vital experiences and on study of the history of the German Workers Movement. This means, among other things, that a considerable number of our citizens, particularly the comrades of the Socialist Unity Party, will express the desire to give their children an atheistic education. Since this circle of people is constantly growing, the conduct of solemn activities for certain events has become a vital necessity. This begins with our smallest children, it passes through entrance into school, and proceeds to Youth Dedication. It experiences its high point in the solemn wedding under state auspices.
>
> The City Council of Suhl has, therefore, taken upon itself the task of arranging solemn Name Givings for our newborn infants; here the opportunity will be offered parents, according to traditional usage, also to name sponsors for their children. Moreover, the factories—which until now have for the most part given presents from their Cultural and Social Funds at a birth—are asked in the future to bring the congratulations and presents of the factory on the occasion of participation in the solemn Name Giving. This Name Giving will be conducted in a most solemn manner, so that it will become a lasting memory for the parents, especially through the appropriate certificate of participation issued by the City Council.
>
> Until further notice the City Council will conduct this Name Giving for all interested parties of the district. Later a Committee for the Conduct of Name Giving will be established in the other cities as well.
>
> The opportunity to participate is being offered children up to one

[20] Cf. "Lebensweihen in Suhl und Neuhaus/R.," *Freies Wort* (Suhl, Thuringia), March 3, 1958.

[21] Werner Mielisch, "Zur Kindesweihe," *Lausitzer Rundschau*, April 24, 1958.

year of age. Should the parents of children even older express the desire to participate, then the Name Giving can take place at any time through the Commissioner for the Office of Personal Statistics connected with the City Council of Suhl. Parents should, however, announce their intention in advance. Since this Name Giving will be a permanent arrangement, the parents may announce at any time, at their convenience. Announcements should be made to Comrade Frau Lischke at the City Hall, Room 17. For the first Name Giving Saturday, February 15, has been set as the deadline for announcements. Should our citizens have any further inquiries Comrade Frau Lischke will be happy to answer them.[22]

Parents and sponsors are reminded of their responsibility to educate the children, from their earliest years, in the spirit of humanism, to become true and useful citizens of the Socialist state. They are told of the sacrifices entailed during the last decade to insure the peace and happiness which the infant is now to enjoy:

At this moment the father of the child or the grandfather (who also served as sponsor) might perhaps have thought of their own childhood, which, under the aura of capitalist exploitation, was in no way beautiful and full of childhood's joys. . . . The best sons of our people have devoted themselves to the happy life of our children— for this the Party of the working class has fought.[23]

It is important to note here that in none of the initiation rites is the theme of purification or rebirth central. In contrast to the Hellenistic mysteries, to Jewish rites of cleansing, and to Christian baptism one finds here an easy and harmonious passage into the great Socialist community, the redeemed community. Today Socialist Name Givings are being promoted vigorously, though Christian baptisms still outnumber them. One Evangelical pastor from the Soviet Zone of Germany has estimated, in a confidential re-

[22] Mayor Kurt Klose in *Freies Wort*, February 8, 1958. Cited in the brochure *Vor der Jugendweihe die Sozialistische Taufe* (Bonn: Bundesministerium für gesamtdeutsche Fragen, n.d. [*ca.* 1958]). The first Name Giving was held on February 23, 1958.

[23] "Klein Petras festlicher Tag," *Freie Presse*, February 18, 1958.

port, that for the years 1957, 1958, and 1959, about seventy per cent of newborn children were baptized, while thirty per cent were brought to the Socialist ceremony. He stated, however, that in some communities these figures are reversed.

Other East European areas—Czechoslovakia, Poland, and Hungary—have recently begun to share the experiences of their German comrades in sponsoring these state rites.[24] In none of these lands are the drives so intense or the stakes so high as in embattled East Germany. But here are some "scenarios" from Hungary for Socialist name-giving and burial services:

> In the hall the Pioneers form a guard of honor. The parents arrive with their infants and are seated in the first row. The table in front is covered with a red cloth and the national flag. . . . The "social registry" of the people's council or the mass organization holding the celebration is on the table. In it, an appropriate text pledges the parents to bring up their children as true Socialist men. . . . Next to the book are the ornately printed certificates for the children. After the first number by the choir, the chairman of the district council gives a seven to eight minute speech. Then he calls upon the parents to sign the oath and hands them the certificates. An approximately eight-year-old Pioneer recites "The Cradle Song" by Attila Jozsef. As many Pioneers as there are babies then present each mother with a bunch of flowers. One Pioneer greets the newborn babies on behalf of all the Pioneers. Then again a number by the choir, followed by a speech by the head of an industrial enterprise who talks on behalf of the 'larger family' and 'the community of the place of work.' This is followed by the distribution of presents and the closing number of the choir (a march with a quick rhythm).

> Where there are facilities for it, those present might drink to the health of the babies and the parents in an adjoining room.

> If possible, an important functionary should deliver the funeral address. The speech should be personal, should deal with the family, those left behind, and should affect the feelings of those present. It is not right that at the funeral of a progressive man dry, seminar-like speeches be made.

> After the funeral address, the procession accompanying the coffin

[24] Cf. "Battle for Belief," *East Europe*, IX, 11 (November, 1960), 13-15.

to the grave should line up in a certain order. On the way to the grave, the choir or orchestra should start a funeral song. At the grave a close friend or colleague of the dead should make a short farewell speech, and to the tunes of a funeral march the coffin should be lowered.[25]

Youth Dedication in East Germany

It is significant to note as we consider the Communist Youth Dedication that the ceremony has been preceded, for both Nazis and Communists, by instruction classes. The East German Youth Dedication today follows a series of ten Youth Sessions, extending over a six-month period, which revolve about the themes of dialectical materialism: the origins of the universe; the evolution of life, including human life, on earth; the development of human society; the struggles of the masses for social progress; proposals for social improvement from Thomas More to Marx, Engels, Lenin, and Khrushchev; the distinctive social and artistic values of Socialist society; and preparation for the Youth Dedication. Throughout the syllabus employed in these lessons human reason is glorified. The child is encouraged to align his thinking, his activities, and his emotions with the pattern of economic and cultural progress as exemplified by the Soviet Union. He is assured that no supernatural powers were involved in the creation of the universe.[26] Rather, one of the principles guiding the first sessions is that "Man is a part of nature which surrounds him. He originated in nature and was originally completely dependent on nature. But he began, step by step, to free himself from the bonds of nature and to become her lord."[27] The effect clearly envisaged in the Youth Sessions is that children will be systematically turned from religious or churchly beliefs.[28] The sessions and the dedication are intended as a bridge which will lead children decisively

---

[25] *Ibid.*, 14-15.

[26] Cf. "Themenplan der Jugendstunden" and "Auszüge aus *Weltall, Erde, Mensch*," U. Jeremias, *Die Jugendweihe in der Sowjetzone* (2nd, enlarged ed.; Bonn: Bundesministerium für gesamtdeutsche Fragen, 1958), pp. 51-70.

[27] *Ibid.*, p. 51.

[28] Cf. Appendix 8, "Extracts from the Speech of the Deputy Premier . . . ."

away from religious distractions and commit them in a solemn, communal rite to unreserved service to the state. It is a bridge toward the formation of the new Socialist man, toward the formation of Socialist consciousness—a consciousness which sets forth a new divinity and the eternal life of the party.

On the basis at once of the anti-Christian history of the Youth Dedication, the materialistic world-view repeatedly bound up with it, and the content of the vow itself as it relates to the total Communist ideology, the bishops of the Evangelical Church immediately responded with an either/or position:

> To the Congregations of the Evangelical Church
> in Berlin-Brandenburg

A "Central Committee for Youth Dedication in the German Democratic Republic" has urged parents whose children will leave school in 1955 to announce them for Youth Dedication. Insofar as this invitation is directed to parents and children who belong to no Christian church we simply have no more to say about the matter.

The invitation to the Youth Dedication in 1955 is, however, directed to *all* young people "irrespective of their world-view." On the basis of the clear and sober differentiation which must be made between the Christian faith and every so-called world-view, we are under obligation to draw the following to the attention of all parents and children who belong to the Evangelical Church:

Already prior to our time, Youth Dedication was established as an affair for those people who renounced the church and its message. There can be no doubt that the newly planned Youth Dedication for 1955 is attached to this old tradition of Youth Dedication. On this point we are in agreement with the convinced adherents of Marxism-Leninism, that the Christian faith and the Marxist world-view stand in an unbridgeable, inner contradiction. For this reason we press for a clear distinction between Christian confirmation and the secular Youth Dedication.

Parents and children must know that the confession of Evangelical faith cannot be brought into harmony with participation in the Youth Dedication. For that reason the ordering of ecclesiastical life in the Evangelical Church in Berlin-Brandenburg in 1954 requires the following:

Children who submit themselves to a ceremony which stands in contradiction to confirmation (Youth Dedication and the like) cannot be confirmed.

Matters stood thus already in the old ordering of our church life.

On the basis of our spiritual responsibility for our confirmands and their parents, we bring this clear statement to the timely consideration of our confirmands. The Lord Jesus Christ has said, "Whoever is not with me is against me."

May he strengthen all of us, particularly our confirmands, in a joyful and fearless confession of him, the sole Lord and Redeemer of our life![29]

The bishops recognized in the Youth Dedication a fundamental decision for or against the Gospel: "Young people who announce themselves for the Youth Dedication cannot be confirmed. They withdraw from the fellowship of those who may participate in the Lord's Supper and exercise the office of godparent."[30] The similarity to confirmation and the outright contradiction is made clear in this "Statement" by Landesbischof Noth of Saxony:

The Youth Dedication can, however, be understood only as a substitute for the church's confirmation. It takes place on a Sunday in April, in the same month during which confirmation is held. Preceding it is a comprehensive preparation embracing ten double-sessions. A certificate is conferred on participants in the Dedication. The Youth Dedication is not intended to be the celebration associated with leaving school, but it is to be an act of consecration, which, so it is affirmed, is to be "a fount of energy for their further development." All of this is manifestly an attempt to copy the church's confirmation.[31]

The Communists themselves insist that the intent of the Youth Dedication is simply the education of children as upright citizens, who will unite in the endeavor to bring about the peace and prosperity of their fatherland. They charge churchmen with instigat-

---

[29] *Kirchliches Jahrbuch* (1954), pp. 146-47.

[30] Encyclical letter of Bishop Otto Dibelius to the pastors and congregations of the Evangelical Church of Berlin-Brandenburg at the beginning of January, 1955, in *Kirchliches Jahrbuch* (1955), p. 112.

[31] *Kirchliches Jahrbuch* (1954), p. 147.

ing unrest among the parents and with inaugurating a split between Christian and non-Christian children. The churchmen ob-
struct the peace and unity of the people.[32] The text of the vow
would not, at first sight, appear too objectionable. In 1957 the
vow read as follows:

Dear young friends!
Are you prepared, as faithful sons and daughters of our Workers'
and Farmers' State, to work and fight for a happy life for the entire
German people, then answer:
    Yes, we vow it!
Are you prepared, with us in common, to devote your entire energy
to the great and noble cause of Socialism, then answer:
    Yes, we vow it!
Are you prepared to work for friendship between peoples, and with
the Soviet people and all peace-loving men of the world to safeguard
and to defend peace, then answer:
    Yes, we vow it!
We have received your vow. You have set yourself a high and noble
goal. You have enlisted in the band of millions of men who work
and fight for peace and Socialism. Solemnly we receive you into the
community of workers in our German Democratic Republic and
promise you support, protection, and aid.[33]

The Christian churches, both Evangelical and Roman Catholic,
have maintained that this is a case of a festive, atheistic confessional act, even if this is not stated as such in the vow itself. The
entire history and circumstance of the Youth Dedication is atheistic, as is indicated by the following pronouncement of the Evangelical bishops of Germany regarding a speech of Walter Ulbricht
on September 29, 1957:

Once again thousands of children in our congregations are preparing themselves to make their confession to our Lord Jesus Christ
in confirmation. At the same time the attempt is being made to win

[32] Cf. the excerpts from the SED (Socialist Unity Party) paper *Das Volk*
(Weimar), February 17, 1955, as reprinted in U. Jeremias, *op. cit.,* p. 71.
[33] *Kirchliches Jahrbuch* (1957), pp. 151-52. This same text remained in use
for the rite in 1958. Cf. *Kirche in der Sowjetzone,* published by Dr. S. Helle
(West Berlin: 1958).

these baptized children of ours for an atheistic Youth Dedication. In such a situation our families are called to a decision and a confession. For here it is simply a matter of either/or. Either a child takes part in the Youth Dedication or in confirmation. It is impossible to combine the two.

Herr Walter Ulbricht, First Secretary of the Central Committee of the SED and First Deputy Chairman of the Praesidium of the Council of Ministers, has once again made this clear in the speech he made on September 29, 1957, at the opening of the Youth Dedication Year in Sonneberg in Thuringia. Previously it was always said: Youth Dedication in the German Democratic Republic in no way signifies a confession to atheism; it is something altogether different from the free thinkers' Youth Dedication of former years. Now Herr Ulbricht has said—and we quote from *Neues Deutschland*—that Youth Dedication is a fine old custom: in West Germany, too, children go to Youth Dedication. And then he tells of his own Youth Dedication in 1907. So it actually is the old institution of the free thinkers which is supposed to supplant the church's confirmation.

The other statements, too, in Herr Ulbricht's speech make this completely clear. He says we should not permit ourselves to be prevented from "throwing overboard old, outworn dogmas." As examples he cites the following in the course of his speech:

A pastor in the vicinity of Leipzig has made his confirmands learn "a confession of faith invented by him." He cites these sentences from the confession: "I believe that God has created me and all creatures. Not what is taught in school, but what the pastor teaches is right." A boy wrote this second sentence in his notebook, not at his pastor's dictation, certainly not as part of "a confession of faith," but out of his own head. The first sentence, however, "I believe that God has created me and . . ." comes, as every Evangelical child knows, from Martin Luther's *Small Catechism* and is among the confessions of our church.

Another example cited by Herr Ulbricht: the young people are required in confirmation instruction to "believe that they have been created by supernatural beings." That we have been created by "supernatural beings"—in the plural!—is not taught in any confirmation instruction. However, we do believe and confess that truth of the First Article, that God has created us and all creatures. With God's help we want to go on believing and confessing this in the future.

A further example cited by Herr Ulbricht is the great German poet Gottfried Herder. Herder indeed stated that a boy must learn natural science—something the church has never questioned, either then or now. But it should be added that Herder gave this School Address in 1798 when he was General Superintendent [of church and school] in Weimar, and that this same speech contains the words: "True religion will never be overthrown; the gates of hell will not prevail against it and the Anti-Christ himself must further it!"

Finally, Herr Ulbricht not only called upon the factories, the Machine and Tractor Stations, the Peoples' Own Department, and the Agricultural Production Communities and the Womens' Committees to support the Youth Dedication. He also required the Popular Education Departments of the Councils, i.e., organs of the state administration, to cooperate in the preparation for the Youth Dedication. This is in contradiction to the declaration given the bishops on December 3, 1956, at the highest state level, namely, that the Youth Dedication is not a matter for the state, but simply for those who desire the Youth Dedication, and that organs of the state are not given the task of putting themselves unreservedly in the service of the Youth Dedication.

We, your bishops, declare: The decision between confirmation and Youth Dedication is a matter involving the souls of your children and the salvation of your own souls. Our answer to the new propaganda for the Youth Dedication and to all attacks against our faith can only be that we take confirmation instruction much more seriously than previously and that we, together with our children, will keep faith the more firmly with God and the church of Jesus Christ.

Threats will not terrify us. During the years of the church's great struggle [under National Socialism] we learned ever and again that God will help his people through all temptations. He will not leave us without his help.

It is written: "We ought to obey God rather than men." And our Savior Jesus Christ has said, "Whosoever therefore shall confess me before men, him will I also confess before my Father which is in heaven."

> Bischof D. Beste, Bischof D. Dibelius, Bischof D. Hornig, Bischof D. Jaenicke, Bischof D. Krummacher, Bischof D. Mitzenheim, Bischof D. Noth, Oberkirchenrat Schröter.[34]

[34] From "An unsere Gemeinden." Reprinted in U. Jeremias, *op. cit.,* pp. 96-98.

The Present Status of the Conflict

More recently Bishop Dibelius announced an altered position with regard to the rites.[35] The same decisive "No" is still given to the Youth Dedication. But greater recognition has been taken of the extreme duress under which parents and children are placed. Though still regarding the vow as at least lip service to atheism and thus a sin, the Evangelical church will, at the discretion of the local pastor, accept those who repent of their participation in the ceremony and admit them to confirmation.[36] The lapse of time involved here is viewed as a pastoral matter, but Bishop Dibelius emphasized that the church must allow time for spiritual reorientation.[37]

The territorial churches of East Germany still regard the "No" to Youth Dedication as rooted in the First Commandment.[38] However, they have subjected the whole inner nature and practice of confirmation to careful reassessment. An effort has been made to avoid the impression of understanding confirmation as a final rite; some time is permitted to elapse between the regular catechetical instruction and the special preparation for the Lord's Supper. The child and his parents are spoken to either individually or in small circles, and the full weight of sin within a hostile world, as well as the rich treasures of God's mercy and the support of the Christian congregation, are brought to the child's attention.[39] Russian Communists have been willing to concede coexistence or a slow death to the church, but German Communism has been characteristically more thoroughgoing. Until recently it was only here among Iron Curtain countries that one found such a dedication rite.[40] In recent years East German authorities have bent their

[35] Cf. the transcript of the television interview with Bishop Dibelius, *Kirchliches Jahrbuch* (1958), p. 192.

[36] Cf. *Time*, January 5, 1959, p. 60.

[37] *Kirchliches Jahrbuch* (1958), p. 193.

[38] Cf. Heins Bernau, "Abendmahlszulassung ohne Abendmahl?" *Junge Kirche*, XXI, 8 (August 10, 1960), 402.

[39] Cf. the conclusions reached by the Synod of the Evangelical Church in Saxony, June 29, 1960, *ibid.*, pp. 400-402.

[40] Cf. Otto Dibelius, *Report to the Evangelical Church in Germany*, p. 3.

efforts to make the rite compulsory for *all* children, not simply for those of non-church families. The campaign in the press has been conducted under the slogan "Youth Dedication for all Children." This crucial vow becomes a means, in addition to the Free German Youth and the public schools, of building a new "official religion."

Roman Catholic children who have participated in the Youth Dedication have been excommunicated by the church, or it is understood that by their participation they have excommunicated themselves. However, the conflict between Youth Dedication and first communion has not been as pronounced as with confirmation, since East Germany has traditionally been Lutheran territory. About eleven per cent of the population is Roman Catholic. It is only since the end of World War II that so many Roman Catholics have settled in this territory, about a million refugees from East Prussia, Silesia, and the Sudetenland.[41]

Figures for participation in the Youth Dedication rite during recent years have been confusing and conflicting. There is evidence to indicate that both the atheists' boasts of triumph and the church's concessions of loss have been misleading.[42] But concentrated efforts for full participation have brought increased results. The following percentages of eighth grade students participating in the dedication present a sobering picture:[43]

[41] "Die Lage der Kirchen in der Sowjetzone," *op. cit.*

[42] For the Evangelical Lutheran Provincial Church of Saxony the *Kirchliches Jahrbuch* (1956), p. 185, gives the percentage of those not confirmed because of the inroads of Youth Dedication as 1.6 for 1955 and 3.6 for 1956 (1,952 children). Some figures triple these percentages.

[43] These are the figures claimed by the East German authorities, according to the report of the Central Committee for Youth Dedication; church leaders in West Germany cast doubt upon the accuracy of some of these figures. The claim is made that 135,000 boys and girls participated in the Youth Dedication in 1960 and that the number rose to 154,774 in 1962. The Bonn correspondent of the *Manchester Guardian* (see note 17 above) comments on the strangulation as follows: "This year only one out of every 10 children of school-leaving age was given church confirmation: 15 years ago four children out of five were confirmed, and only 4 per cent of the people of Eastern Germany were registered as having no religion."

```
1957 . . . . . . . . . . . 25.0%
1958 . . . . . . . . . . . 44.1%
1959 . . . . . . . . . . . 80.4%
1960 . . . . . . . . . . . 88.0%
1961 . . . . . . . . . . . 90.0%
1962 . . . . . . . . . . . 90.4%
1963 . . . . . . . . . . . 90.6%
```

In some communities almost every child goes through Youth Dedication, whereas in others almost all are confirmed.[44] Yet 1,600 Protestant and Roman Catholic teachers fled East Germany (before the erection of the Berlin Wall) to avoid the moral compromise of encouraging their pupils to participate in the Youth Dedication.

Many children who have been sent, under pressure, to Youth Dedication are later sent by their parents to confirmation and Holy Communion. Church authorities attempt to give due recognition to the duress under which children and parents are placed.

It is to the teachers that responsibility is channeled to gain one hundred per cent participation in the ceremony. Roman Catholic participation has been lower, with 28 to 45 per cent of those leaving school participating in 1959. These percentages rose to from 45 to 59 per cent for 1960. Yet 29 to 30 per cent of these found their way back to Roman Catholic life after a trial period.[45] It should be added that the Communists anticipate that the percentages achieved in connection with Youth Dedication may later be reflected in Socialist weddings and in the number of children presented for Name Giving rather than for Christian baptism.

Youth Dedication and the Rite of Confirmation

The timing of the *Verpflichtungsfeier* of the Nazis and the *Jugendweihe* of the Communists coincides with a turning point in the career of a German youth. Confirmation marks the end of

---

[44] *Kirchliches Jahrbuch* (1958), p. 193.
[45] *Die katholische Kirche in Berlin und Mitteldeutschland*, pp. 44-45.

school for many, the transition to secondary school for others. It is understood to mark the beginning of a certain spiritual maturity and independence. At this moment a decision is required regarding the youth's plans for the future. It marks the occasion for a great family gathering, a festive celebration, with many presents, particularly from the sponsors, with flowers, and congratulatory cards. It is an ideal moment for a decision regarding faith in God—or in the Führer, or the workers' state. For the Youth Dedication stores have featured the same black suits, white shirts, and black ties usually worn for confirmation. Moreover, after the new vow of allegiance and kissing of the red flag there have been the same token gifts, for example, a small sum of money, or a wrist watch.

In German cultural life confirmation has occupied a unique place. It is often much more a family event than a Christian celebration.[46] It is at this point that the German *Volkskirche* is most *volkstümlich,* and this event offers the most outstanding opportunity for the ideologies to capitalize upon *volkstümliches Gebrauch* ("popular custom"). The Communists contend that the vow does not induct one into a religious fellowship, that it is a social and political event, that it is a festive induction into the community of mature men and women and is in no way directed against the churches. It does not conflict with religious commitment, so it is held, but is rather a "promise," a "clarification of will" rather than an "expression of faith." The ceremony is to be applicable to all circles of the populace, "irrespective of their world-view and their religious convictions." The claim is made that it is motivated by a spirit of tolerance rather than by opposition to religion; the church's stand against the ceremony, on the other

---

[46] The same observation applies, but with less force, to baptism. Günter Jacob states, in his "Situation of the Evangelical Church in East Germany" (translated from *Dokumente* [June, 1957] in *Cross Currents,* VII [1957], 335): "We have done away with home baptisms, a practice which has led to 'the transformation of baptism into a feast of the consecration of life and individual family happiness.'" These differences surrounding Name Giving and Youth Dedication have practically brought to an end the *volkskirchliche* character of the East German church.

hand, has been characterized as an effort to divert attention from the decisive question of peace.

However, in view of the continual relegation of the Christian faith to the sphere of "superstition," "antipathy to science," and "religious prejudice," and in view of the many refusals to allow young people to continue their studies "on the excuse of insufficient political and social activity,"[47] this façade of easy compatibility becomes transparent indeed. Children who have persisted in attending confirmation instruction have been ridiculed and mishandled. They have been debarred from employment. It should be added that the East German regime is fully aware that by debarring young men and women from entrance into high schools, technical schools, universities, and seminaries it is invoking the most dreaded penalty short of imprisonment. It restricts the development of latent powers and deprives young people from participation in their world.

The Significance of the Socialist Vow

Several points, finally, should be noted regarding the significance of Youth Dedication.

First, it is believed by the representatives of an ideology that a well-developed, "solemn" cult is an essential means for promoting the ideology. So long as these traditional ceremonies, with all the family associations that cluster about them, remain the exclusive property of the church, the ideology is at a serious disadvantage in promulgating its cause. The totalitarian regimes are aware that with regard to the milestones of life—birth, puberty, marriage, and death—they can offer only a paucity of ritual in comparison with the hoary traditions of the church.[48] They are confronted with the

---

[47] Günter Jacob, *Das Licht Scheint in der Finsternis* (Stuttgart: Evangelisches Verlagswerk, 1954), p. 95.

[48] It is interesting to note that, as Hegel points out in *The Philosophy of History* (New York: Dover Publications, 1956), p. 292, we owe the introduction of solemn promises and vows especially to the Romans. Hegel also emphasizes, as one of the characteristic features of Roman religion, the extent to which the *sacra* are exploited as means of furthering the purposes of a youthful state (cf. pp. 284 ff.).

hard fact that personal and family life remain spheres of freedom attached to the church rather than to the ideology. The rites of the church have an appeal rooted in the past of families and relationships; new symbols have for the most part failed to reorient life's meaning and values about the new "sacred" centers.[49] Only by surrounding its own ideas with the emotional coloring of religion will the ideology be able to capture the allegiance of the masses. A new religious tradition is formed as the foundation for a new society and a new culture. An order is to be built on a strictly "scientific" foundation, in contrast to the "superstitious" Christian framework.

Second, a public pledge becomes an aid to the wavering resolution and conviction of the novice. It is understood to be a "declaration of loyalty" to the workers' and farmers' state; it will also safeguard the initiate from relapsing into the bourgeois attitudes and values which characterized his parents. The Italian Fascists required an oath of each person who joined the party, binding him "to obey without question the commands of the Duce . . . and when necessary to shed his blood for the Fascist revolution."[50] In the Third Reich it was understood that the ideal type, the SS man, through his oath to the person of Adolf Hitler had become more than a soldier: he was "the exemplary bearer of the idea of Adolf Hitler."[51] For the *Wehrmacht* conscripts, the oath of allegiance to the person of the Führer served to check the power of the generals.

Third, such a vow is an early form of accepting the responsibility for interiorizing the culture. With it the initiate enters into the community of workers. He not only indicates an intellectual acceptance of the values and objectives of the community. More

---

[49] Cf. the call by Leonid Ilichev, Russian party propaganda chief, for new civic rituals. George Bailey, "Religion in the Soviet Union," *The Reporter,* July 16, 1964, p. 27.

[50] Erwin von Beckerath, "Fascism," *Encyclopedia of the Social Sciences,* ed. Edwin R. A. Seligman (New York: Macmillan, 1935), VI, 136.

[51] Cf. partial translation of Document 3429-PS, "The SS Calls You," *Nazi Conspiracy and Aggression,* VI, 135. Cf. also Franz Neumann, *Behemoth: The Structure and Practice of National Socialism* (New York: Oxford University Press, 1942), pp. 84-85.

important, he is led to a profound emotional identification with these supreme realities. In a sense, the youth is told at a most impressionable age, "Now you have become a full-fledged member of the new Socialist order. In this initiation the tribe transfers its vision and its command to you. You dare not be inadequate before the challenge facing you." Thus the rite is of profound significance not only for the individual but for the entire society. The initiate is not only given prerogatives. At a particular, determinable time and place the individual is inducted into the responsibilities of a well-integrated, technical society.[52]

Fourth, the rite is to create the courage required to overcome the anxieties faced even in a collective culture. It combats the emptiness and meaninglessness which are the special forms of anxiety in the modern world.[53] It does this by defining an individual's passage from one mode of existence to another. Now his place in society is made certain through a spiritual experience.

Fifth, the ceremony serves as a "witness," or as a means of propaganda. It witnesses to the formation of the "new man" of Communism and to the "new morality" the ideology espouses. Those who oppose the rites of Socialism are against morality, truth, and Socialism, as one of Walter Ulbricht's slogans reads: "He alone acts morally and humanely who actively devotes himself to the victory of Socialism." The East German government has found it necessary to win in this struggle because of the prominence attached to it in the ideological conflict. The press has made such an issue of participation in the Youth Dedication, in part because of the either/or stand of the majority of German bishops, that it could not afford to concede defeat on such an issue.

Sixth, the vow demonstrates the continuing relationship of Marxism as a politico-economic theory to its philosophical basis, dialectical materialism. There are many who insist that the philo-

[52] Cf. "Entwurf des Jugendgesetzes," *Junge Welt*, XVII, 229A (September 28/29, 1963), 3-5.
[53] Cf. Paul Tillich, *The Courage To Be* (New Haven: Yale University Press, 1959), p. 43.

sophical aspirations of Communism are merely incidental, that its essential nature lies in being a movement toward social reform. However, here one clearly sees it as more than a political alternative; it is an answer to the "why," the "whence," and "whither" of life.

It is significant to note also the timing of these ceremonies. The direct conflict with Christian worship under the Nazis was to be seen in the film hour for children on Sunday mornings; on these occasions the children were exhorted to be ready for heroic sacrifices, and they sang soul-stirring, patriotic songs. On many occasions Communist Name Givings, Youth Dedications, and mass meetings have been staged on Sunday mornings designedly to conflict with Christian services or festivals, for example, Easter or Pentecost. Communist hero-worship and utilization of renovated Christian rites fail to harmonize with the vigorous Communist denunciation of Christian, Democratic, and Fascist "irrationalism" in this area. However, except for 1955, the first year in which Youth Dedication was refurbished in East Germany, direct conflict with the traditional date for Christian confirmation, Palm Sunday, has been avoided.

One should not, moreover, overlook the significance of the gifts enjoined in Nazi as well as Communist rites. A gift of one hundred marks, as described in Appendix 9, provides no little incentive for opportunists to participate in a Name Giving. Yet with all the advantages accruing to parents and participants, only a very small percentage of participants takes the oaths with the desired seriousness.

A common feature of these ceremonies is that they draw upon the cultural heritage of the participants as far as possible. Familiar tunes, phrases, and customs are retained and new meanings are injected into them. In addition to the relatives who are invited, leading figures from public life, from the teaching profession, the arts, and industrial life, are invited to participate in order to provide an atmosphere of legitimacy and acceptance. Behind all of these stands the party organization, lending its direct or indirect support.[54]

Yet in all these rites of the ideologies one feature must strike the Christian as most pronounced: the lack of originality, the lifeless imitation which characterize Nazi as well as Communist ceremonies. Instead of demonstrating a creative or imaginative "resymbolizing" of the events of life, they have, in spite of allegations to the contrary, simply succeeded in aping what the church does more convincingly. The lack of life which St. John associates in his Gospel with the cosmos apart from Christ is illustrated most vividly here.

Socialist Marriage and Burial Services

The promotion of these civic ceremonies forms the most recent chapter in the borrowing of political symbols from the religious tradition. Marriage ceremonies and funeral rites consecrate these key situations in life in obedience to orthodox ideology and the sacred state. The tables adorned with candles and flowers and standing before busts or pictures of leaders have certain inescapable connections with the arrangement of the Christian altar. Many terms employed in the rites have been taken directly from Christian orders of worship. The decision to choose between a church wedding or a secular wedding faces young couples in all the Iron Curtain countries, and it is not surprising to learn that the number of church weddings has decreased sharply in East Germany. One must admit, however, that the choice of a church wedding is often based on the festivities attendant on the traditional community celebration. Much that was earlier held to be "Christian" in German cultural life is now clearly seen to be social tradition and custom.

---

[54] It is significant to note that Youth Dedication has ostensibly been promoted by a private organization, the "Commission for the Consecration of East German Youth"; but the weight of party organization and state officialdom clearly stands behind the disarming front, as the speeches of Walter Ulbricht and Otto Grotewohl make clear.

Socialist burial services have not been fully organized as yet; the event of death has an individual and personal character not present in the course of life, and it is here that God and eternal life inevitably merge. Yet Communist authorities have announced their readiness to have party functionaries speak at the grave of the deceased.[55] In contrast to the central thought of the Christian funeral, the expectation of the resurrection of the dead, the Socialist burial service is understood to be an "act of inner strengthening for the survivors."[56] The endeavors of the deceased for the building of a Socialist community are to be commemorated and valued here "in all their heights and depths."[57]

These solemn vows remind Christians of the abuses in the administration of the sacraments by the churches over the centuries. When churches offer ten distinct classes of funerals, with prices graded accordingly, Christians will become cynical.[58] When first-, second-, and third-class weddings are promoted, many will be disgusted with anything the church offers. But these vows, revolving as they do about economic and political security, point directly to the supreme concern, beyond all gods and altars, of the Communist movement. They reveal unmistakably that the party sets itself up in place of the Christian church.

[55] Bishop Dibelius has declared, for example: "I have visited, for instance, a township where a population of some 7,000 is traditionally ministered to by two pastors. Now, however, the two pastors are confronted by the counter-officiating of five secular orators whose services are recommended by the official local gazettes." *Report to the Evangelical Church in Germany*, p. 5.

[56] "Sozialistische Bestattung," reported by the German news agency, Informationsbüro West (Berlin-Schlachtensee), June 5, 1959.

[57] *Ibid.* Cf. also Appendix 2, "Basic Considerations . . . in Stalinstadt."

[58] Cf. *Time*, December 7, 1962, pp. 53-54.

6

IDEOLOGY AND THE QUESTION OF TRUTH

> . . . THE *myths are not descriptions of things, but expressions of a determination to act.*
>
> GEORGES SOREL, *Reflections on Violence*
> (1908)

Few words which enjoyed the propitious beginnings once surrounding "ideology" have been so quickly and thoroughly defamed. Destutt de Tracy coined it in the period of the French Revolution to describe a "science of ideas," a philosophical discipline which was to form the base for an entire framework of the sciences. But Napoleon Bonaparte denounced it as the product of a theoretical attitude which fails to square with reality, particularly with the social and political situation. Napoleon did not, however, understand ideology to be simply otherworldly; had this been the case, he would never have denounced it so vigorously. He suggested that ideology as theory possesses a decisive relation to concrete political practice.[1] In place of de Tracy's philosophical use of the term for the anthropological and psychological base of the cultural sciences, Napoleon's contemptuous twist, calling the group of philosophers who opposed his imperial ambitions "ideologists," has to this day impressed its derisive stamp on the word.[2]

Though he did not use the term "ideology," Francis Bacon had earlier reflected on men's rationalizations in his famous essay on "idols." He was well aware of the persistent way in which subjectivity, prejudice, propaganda, and comprehensive systems lead men into illusion. In all previous attempts to arrive at true knowl-

---

[1] Hans Barth, *Wahrheit und Ideologie* (Zürich: Manesse Verlag, 1945), p. 15.
[2] Karl Mannheim, *Ideology and Utopia,* trans. Louis Wirth and Edward Shils (London: Routledge and Kegan Paul, Ltd., and New York: Harcourt, Brace and Co., 1936), p. 72.

edge Bacon detected many "phantoms" or sources of error—idols of the tribe, of the cave, the market, and the theater. Particularly in the latter he anticipates the ideologies. Idols of the theater are "so many stage plays, representing worlds of their own creation after an unreal and scenic fashion."[3]

Karl Marx and the Destruction of Ideology

Karl Marx attached himself to the tradition, running from Napoleon to Spengler, which distinguishes between the doer and the contemplator.[4] He called an "ideology" every theory which attempts simply to *explain* reality without willing to transform it. An ideology, he said, serves both to mask and to justify evils in a particular situation. His interest was not in "interpreting" the world, as he saw this done by Hegel. He was interested in transforming it.[5] He claimed to have overcome the alienation between theory and practice. Hegel had up-ended man, had set him on his head by making the Spirit basic. Marx was simply returning man to a solid footing by setting him on his feet again.

For Marx, law, politics, religion, "bourgeois" science are all "ideologies" shielding the interests of the privileged classes. The propertied classes have created these superstructures to mask the class struggle going on in the economic sphere, the "substructure" below. The ideologies cannot be termed "true." They serve merely to justify and idealize the privileges of the exploiting classes. They are rationalizations of the economic interests of the ruling group in a society: they are dangerous because those who create them are not conscious of what is actually occurring; they have a measure

---

[3] *Novum Organum,* Aphorism XLIV.

[4] Cf. Hans Barth, *op. cit.,* pp. 15-16.

[5] "Theses on Feuerbach," XI. Karl Marx and Friedrich Engels, *Basic Writings on Politics and Philosophy,* p. 245. The manner in which this concern can be said to characterize the Communist movement is illustrated by Ch'en, the terrorist, in André Malraux, *Man's Fate,* trans. Haakon M. Chevalier (New York: Modern Library, 1934), p. 177. Ch'en does not care to account for human suffering; his concern is to diminish it.

of independent development, but the economic aspect will always emerge. Engels writes:

> Political, juridical, philosophical, religious, literary, artistic, etc., development is based on economic development. But all these react upon one another and also upon the economic basis. It is not that the economic situation is *cause, solely* active, while everything else is only passive effect. There is, rather, interaction on the basis of economic necessity, which ultimately always asserts itself.[6]

The ideologies lack any inherent relationship to the modes and relations of production. Their claim to clarify life-situations is a patent deception. Certainly, the assertion that they understand and explain is always made by the ideologies. But the "real motives" of the ideologist are hidden from him, since they are twisted by his class interest:

> Ideology is a process accomplished by the so-called thinker consciously, it is true, but with a false consciousness. The real motive forces impelling him remain unknown to him; otherwise it simply would not be an ideological process. Hence he imagines false or seeming motive forces.[7]

Karl Marx brought into sharp focus the nebulous world of ideas—the representations or images—between the existing subject and the economic and social forces one tries, by means of these ideas, to understand. He could concede no independent truth to these representations, symbols, and concepts. Thus religion is a form of escape for the victims of exploitation. In conformity with the original process of masking, it drains off energies from serious efforts to transform the existing order. The socialist thinker, on the other hand, never permits obsolete ideas to form a part of his philosophy, because socialist philosophy always discards obsolete and valueless ideas.

Marxists, non-Marxists, and anti-Marxists alike have worked

---

[6] "Letter to Heinz Starkenburg, January 25, 1894," Karl Marx and Friedrich Engels, *op cit.,* pp. 410-11.

[7] Engels, "Letter to Franz Mehring, July 14, 1893," *ibid.,* p. 408.

with his concept of surplus value, the socialization of the means of production in large-scale industry, and with his means of tying action to theory. As a tool for the examination of social and economic problems Marx's thought has demonstrated its positive value. An intellectual unveiling was accomplished by Marx. He made a penetrating analysis of the material factors underlying our cultural life. Indeed, we can understand the attractiveness of Communism in under-developed countries only through recourse to Marx's material basis of culture.

Ideology and the Sacrifice of Discussion

However, Marxists have turned Marx's thought into an all-embracing historical and philosophical system. They have claimed universal validity for its "scientific" insights. It is no longer a method of inquiry into political and economic questions but a total explanation for all possible questions. Since they are in dogmatic possession of the truth, Marxists need no longer participate in the sober investigations of the social sciences in order to discover the truth. A symbol system is pawned off and received as fact. It is this dogmatic sense of possession that explains Marxist fanaticism.[8]

Again and again one finds that the price paid for the adoption of an ideology is the sacrifice of discussion. Karl Jaspers summarizes the process in a succinct manner:

> What matters is not what you believe, but that you believe. This is a wonderful perversion. Faith becomes faith in faith. . . . One seizes upon old words like honor, patriotism, loyalty, but at the same time sacrifices everything to the machine, to orders from above, to terror, thus showing that all these words were mere props.[9]

[8] Karl Jaspers, *Way to Wisdom*, trans. Ralph Manheim (New Haven: Yale University Press, 1951), pp. 154-56.

[9] Karl Jaspers, *The Perennial Scope of Philosophy*, trans. Ralph Manheim (New York: Philosophical Library, 1949), pp. 162-63. Note the Nazi "Morning Celebration and Worship Service" in the previous chapter, pp. 102-04, and its celebration of loyalty.

Enthusiasm and ceremonial repetition of slogans replace a dialogue between parties. This sacrifice of free inquiry and discussion in favor of an unquestioned sense of possessing the truth is a feature of every totalitarian regime. In no area is the contrast between the open society and totalitarianism so plain as in their respective views of truth.

One cannot escape the derogatory sense connected with the term "ideology," either in political usage or in that of the social scientist. An aura of self-interest and irrationality looms about the word, and this has destroyed its usefulness in many realms of discourse. Nietzsche, for example, understood knowledge and thought as "falsifying transformations" of a reality which is many-sided and numberless. For him knowledge was both a tool of the will to power and one of its products.[10] It is this struggle for power, he said, that actually stands behind all our conscious motives. It is expressed in the "slave morality" of Christianity as the resentment of a cramped and conventional piety. Karl Mannheim reinterpreted ideology to cover thinking which enables one to act in a situation, and he has pointed to other factors (e.g., the social group) which influence thought. Again, one may see ideology in terms of the definition given by Lasswell and Kaplan: "The *ideology* is the political myth functioning to preserve the social structure."[11] Still the marks of sociological resentment and frustration always cling to the ideologies. The ambiguities and exaggerations associated with the ideologies, the emotional load they usually carry, the selfish interest always visible in their proponents—these account for some of the baser connotations of the word.

But whether or not one is ready to take seriously the possibility of truth in the great ideologies, the *claim* to truth is always made. They are quite unwilling to present themselves merely as tendential approaches to social and political questions. Lenin revealed the orthodox Communist quest for truth and abhorrence of error

---

[10] Hans Barth, *op. cit.,* p. 231.

[11] Harold D. Lasswell and Abraham Kaplan, *Power and Society* (New Haven: Yale University Press, 1950), p. 123.

when at the London Congress of Social Democrats in 1903 he castigated all deviation from "the objective truth" of Marxist doctrine. One cannot avoid the question of truth with regard to the claims either of religion or of the ideologies, though in both cases the desire to avoid the question is continually present. Nazi racism posited as "true" its tenets of the purity and superiority of Aryan blood. Marxist-Leninist philosophy maintains as "true" its interpretation of the course of all previous and subsequent history and its understanding of the nature of science.

Mythical Features and Ideology

Mythical features, where myth is understood as a form of symbolic expression used to objectify social emotions, are common to all the ideologies. The myth has a logic of its own, and it is quite impervious to the examination of reason. It lays claim to its own consistency, and it defies attempts to undermine or upset this consistency. Moreover, myth lays claim to validity on the field of experience, and this can be said of Nazism, Communism, Conservatism, Liberalism, or Fascism. Myth is not simply poetry, for, unlike poetry, it does not justify itself in its own right but continually points beyond itself to fulfillment in action. It has little concern for careful analysis and observation. Whereas argument presupposes, even requires, opposing points of view, the political myth excludes opposite views. Whereas argument proceeds on the basis of thesis and antithesis and even forces opposition to its extreme elements before it is content with synthesis, political myth leads away from the *res* of the matter to illusory solutions.

However, a philosopher of the stature of Plato, while using the dialectical method to test premises, to demonstrate the inadequacies of unexamined opinions, to rise on the ladder of truth, yet found it necessary to insert distinctive myths into his dialogues in order to express nuances of perception which were not amenable to argument. Were we to examine the truth claims of the ideologies simply on the basis of mythical (understood as non-cognitive) and analytical (understood as cognitive) expression we would find that this distinction would necessarily break down before Plato's philosophy. Aristotle, too, suggests that "poetry is something more philosophic and of graver import than history, since its statements are of the nature rather of universals, whereas those of history are singulars."[12] However, in the face of the ideologies today it is highly important to know whether an idea leads to reality or merely occasions an emotional response to an illusory reality. As Cassirer has pointed out, Plato forsook myth in the sphere of political life in favor of understanding.[13] His dialectic is actually designed to examine the distinctive nature and basis of the state.

Yet the senses in which the term "myth" is used are so varied that some differentiation is necessary before we proceed further to speak of the ideologies as "political myths." One may distinguish the following categories:

A. *The ontological myth,* a narrative dealing with the perennial questions: "Where did we come from?" "What is our role here?" "What is our destiny?" The myth in this sense precedes all analytical discourse; it attempts to interpret the basic aspects of human experience in a form both more profound and more universal than propositions of fact or philosophical discourse permit. These are myths in the primary sense of the word: they are man's earliest form of imaginative thought and feeling, the mother-tongue of all mankind. A world-view is embraced in such a comprehensive structure. The myth in this sense is a means of describing the ontological fact that something of this world reaches beyond this world. It is not simply an incredible tale concerning divine beings. Within this understanding, a myth always stands in a special relation to the transcendent reality: it embodies a certain transcendent truth. While forsaking "literal" truth it employs mythological language to refer to a reality "beyond" the richness and variety of sense experience. Though the myth lacks precision and is subject to conflicting interpretations, it communicates in-

[12] *Poetics,* Chap. 9, *Basic Works of Aristotle,* ed. Richard McKeon (New York: Random House, 1941), p. 1464.
[13] Ernst Cassirer, *The Myth of the State* (Garden City: Doubleday Anchor Books, 1955), pp. 74 ff.

sights into the realms of nature and man which could never be stated as adequately by discursive reason.

In its original power, the ontological myth is no longer accessible to sophisticated Western man. Often, however, these old myths may be repeated by poets and philosophers in a completely new context. Or, as shown in Plato's dialogues, a myth may be invented as a means of communicating some measure of a man's thought beyond the circle of his pupils to the multitude.

B. *The spontaneous myth,* arising from the life and experience of a people. This type may be seen in the legends surrounding Paul Bunyan, Daniel Boone, or other folk heroes. In contrast to the foregoing type, the spontaneous myth is a sophisticated achievement, and the ontological insight does not emerge here.

C. *The myth of cultural integration.* The culture of a nation must be integrated by its religion or by some new mythology. The myths of the Boston Tea Party, of Paul Revere, and of Washington at Valley Forge are part of the collective myth of America. In other epochs and other societies religion integrated the religious and political dualities, or the two spheres may have been considered as essentially one. The ideologies respond to the nostalgia for such a long-lost unity. Democracy, too, was deeply indebted in its origins to the Christian faith and to the Christian churches, but there is sufficient evidence on record to indicate that democracy is not now bound inextricably to the Christian faith.

Walter Bagehot has called attention to the happy British solution of clearly differentiating between the efficient elements of political institutions and their theatrical elements.[14] The symbolism revolving about the British crown has helped thwart a serious threat from Fascism and Communism and would function similarly against any other ideology. This medieval anachronism has provided a center of cultural integration superior to blood or Marxist dogma. British Fascism has, indeed, been strongly represented in

[14] James Luther Adams has applied Bagehot's division constructively to the concept of ideology and to religious systems. See his "Religion and the Ideologies," *Confluence,* IV, 1 (April, 1955) 72-84.

politics, but the institution of monarchy has been too vital to allow it to become a threat. The noble lines of Kipling's "Recessional" reminded the English of the dependent status of their world dominion. The pretensions of Queen Victoria's sway were slackened by a remarkable restraint. Kipling could pray the "Judge of Nations" to spare England yet. He reminded the oligarchic Victorian Age of the fate of Nineveh and Tyre, and he invoked the God of history—"lest we forget."

The well-known symbols making up the American mythology—the national anthem, the flag, George Washington, the Constitution, Independence Hall—are not envisioned as eliciting a religious devotion any more than Norse mythology and folklore are recounted the spiritual center for modern Norsemen. They are ceremonial in function. In their function they are far closer to poetry than to dogma. Yet such myths of cultural integration *may* serve to shut off from any transcendent source of authority and they *may* become sacred in their own right. When no transcendent reality is recognized as distinct from the nation, judging events in history, democratic myths and symbols *may* assume sacred pretensions, but predominantly they have served to unify a democratic *polis*.

D. *A point of view* on social and political questions, based on practical arguments and considerations. This kind of stance is distinguished by its tentative nature and presupposes an active party system. It is content to work in terms of strictly limited circumstances and objectives. In place of agreement on questions of origin and destiny it is content to work toward agreement on matters of present policy. Such a point of view may be called an ideology, but, if so, the limited and specific matrix of this thinking should be kept in mind. There is no single, authoritative theory defining the nature of democracy, dissent from which launches one into heterodoxy. But there is a way of governing, a *praxis*. Bound up with this way of governing is a practical program of action, and this has been the normal procedure in the Anglo-Saxon countries. In these countries little enthusiasm has been generated for

the *Weltanschauungsstaat.* The all-inclusive *Weltanschauung* furnishes little help amid the realities of social struggle. The ideologies present an over-simple picture of a situation. They fail to
do justice to the profusion of life. Students of government have
been forced to develop their discipline in terms of a more rigor-
ous social science rather than in the direction of a comprehensive
system. In this procedure, the gathering of statistical data and the
study of day-to-day decision-making have become central.

However, whenever in a democracy one finds discussion with
those of opposite views being obstructed one is witnessing the transformation of democracy, too, into an ideology, a faith. It is for
this reason that the "democratic ideology" cannot be proclaimed as
readily as some of its advocates suggest. The advocates of an ideological crusade against Communism would forge a doctrine of democracy rather than a *praxis.* Certainly one can point to democratic ideals, such as representation of the people, constitutional
safeguards, the two-party system, protection of minorities, individual
freedom and dignity. But the heart of democracy lies in its day-to-
day operation rather than in a doctrinaire faith. It remains a great
experiment, alien to creedal affirmations and declarations of ultimate loyalties.[15]

E. *Limited ideologies,* a system of ideas stemming from personal, occupational, class, or national interest, but laying no claim
to answering questions regarding the whence and whither of life
itself. These ideologies interpret the role of a particular group
within a nation to themselves and to other groups. They also justify the special interests of this group. In this sense the "American
business creed" is an ideology seen as a "response to strain."[16] The
"myth of the common man" and the "myth of the boy apprentice"
would also belong to this category.[17]

[15] Cf. Talmon's contrast between liberal and totalitarian democracy in his *Origins of Totalitarian Democracy,* pp. 1 ff.

[16] F. X. Sutton, S. E. Harris, Carl Kaysen, and James Tobin, *The American
Business Creed* (Cambridge, Mass.: Harvard University Press, 1956), p. 308.

[17] Cf., e.g., Richard Myers, "Myth and Status Systems in Industry," *Reader in
Bureaucracy,* pp. 273-281.

F. *Ideologies embracing a total view of man and society.* Here an interpretation of man and of life is elevated into a faith. Some limited object or entity is given ultimate loyalty. A similarity to the ontological myth is apparent in the concern for the origin, essential nature, and manifest destiny of the group. Heinrich Himmler declared that the SS man was not concerned with "everyday problems" but with "ideological questions of importance for decades and centuries, so that the man . . . knows he is working for a great task which occurs but once in 2,000 years."[18] Such ideologies are elaborated into what is held to be a self-consistent, logical, and scientific system. But by their very nature they cannot be scientific. And reason no longer checks the process of myth making: key tenets become doctrinaire concepts and messianic pretensions appear. A limited or relative truth is glorified because of its value in extending the interests of some group. This is what Maxim Gorky pointed out with reference to Communism: "Rivers of blood have been shed for this sacred idea."

In this sense ideologies are attempts to dominate chaos. They offer global panaceas for local frustrations; they furnish answers to failing social and individual purpose; they offer restitution to workers cheated of their economic birthright and to men deprived of national dignity. But in doing so they oversimplify issues; for example, the productive capacity of labor becomes the key to the understanding of history, or the concept of race becomes the substructure for social and biological science. Always the idea is supposed to possess a logic of its own which renders it beyond question; all opposition, which would call conflicting parties to examine objective data in the spirit of free inquiry, is precluded. The first and basic requirement for truth, the adequacy of an idea in one's mind or of a proposition to reality or actual situations, is surrendered before it is applied. So ideologies in this sense lead away from reality into the realm of aroused feelings and actions rather than deep into the nature of reality.

[18] Quoted in *Nazi Conspiracy and Aggression*, IV, 616.

Ideologies and the Pragmatic Test of Truth

In accordance with these features ideologies become triggers for action, and their social significance is so immense because they call to joint action. They easily become means of asserting power and of extending power over neighboring peoples who may have a less cogent or coherent ideology. Such ideological conquests have represented more significant achievements than military success or victories at plebiscites. In the Christian framework, following the decisive insights of both Plato and Aristotle on this question, thought precedes action, the *bios theoretikos* takes precedence over the *bios politikos*.[19] But for Marx *action,* of one piece with the pragmatism and functionalism common to the Western world, became dominant in knowledge. Since Karl Marx refused to separate the sphere of political action from its theoretical source the emphasis of orthodox Marxists on theoretical competence for all revolutionaries is understandable. The Christian churches, on the other hand, have no specific program for action, and consequently they lack the precision in action which Communism possesses. But they do have resources affording them a unique dynamic in social action. They can hope to have responsible members, sensitive to political and social questions, and possessing the spiritual dynamic with which to deal with them.

It is in the nature of the ideologies that they rest on the pragmatic test of truth: they are true because they are functional; they become true in action. Karl Mannheim draws attention to the pragmatic framework of the ideologies:

> The history of the concept of ideology from Napoleon to Marxism, despite changes in content, has retained the same political criterion of reality. This historical example shows, at the same time, that the pragmatic point of view was already implicit in the accusation which Napoleon hurled at his adversaries. Indeed we may say that for modern man pragmatism has, so to speak, become in some respects, the inevitable and appropriate outlook, and that philosophy in this

[19] Cf. Hannah Arendt, "Tradition and the Modern Age, IV," *Partisan Review,* XXI, 1 (January-February, 1954), 69-75.

case has simply appropriated this outlook and from it proceeded to its logical conclusion.[20]

Again we may note a similarity between the history of the ideologies and the nature of Roman *religio*. What Charles Cochrane states of ancient Rome is directly applicable to the rites of the ideologies: ". . . to say this is to suggest that the spirit of official religion was utterly pragmatic. Accordingly it becomes purely irrelevant to inquire into its substantial truth or falsehood."[21]

In Dewey's instrumentalism, too, ideas are instruments with which men change the world: their instrumental adequacy, that is, their truth or falsity, can be ascertained only in experience, by the degree with which they operate successfully. On this basis the Deweyite group opposed all ultimate metaphysical and theological affirmations. The functionalist interpretation of religion sponsored by Edward Scribner Ames, too, identified religion with the social interest. Ames asserted that "the man who enters thoroughly into the social movements of his time is to that extent thoroughly religious though he may characterize himself otherwise."[22] An idea which continues to work successfully is "true," and when it no longer works it can be declared "false."

This approach to the political myth has been accompanied by devious devices to reassure people that the old conception of truth still prevails. The Nazis reassured the German people that they were being governed on the basis of the firmest loyalty to principles.[23] Yet Hitler distinguished keenly between thought and action, idea and practice, program-maker and practical politician.[24]

---

[20] Karl Mannheim, *op. cit.,* p. 73.

[21] *Christianity and Classical Culture* (New York: Oxford University Press, 1944), p. 101.

[22] *The Psychology of Religious Experience* (New York: Houghton, Mifflin Co., 1910), p. 358.

[23] Cf. Julius Kraft, "Theologische und juristische Formen modernen politischen Wunderglaubens," *Vierteljahreshefte für Zeitgeschichte,* V, 2 (1957), 176 ff.

[24] Cf. Hans Buchheim, *Glaubenskrise im dritten Reich* (Stuttgart: Deutsche Verlags-Anstalt, 1953), pp. 15-16.

To the program-maker belonged "the abstractly correct spiritual conception," but in the heat of battle stood the politician who must deal with political expediency, the man who supplied elastic adjustments geared to concrete action:

> And so an eternal ideal, serving as the guiding star of mankind, must unfortunately resign itself to taking the weaknesses of this mankind into consideration, if it wants to avoid shipwreck at the very outset on the shoals of general human inadequacy. To draw from the realm of the eternally true and ideal that which is humanly possible for small mortals, and make it take form, the search after truth must be coupled with knowledge of the people's psyche.[25]

The validation which Marx accepted is stated in the second thesis on Feuerbach:

> The question whether objective (*gegenständliche*) truth can be attributed to human thinking is not a question of theory, but is a *practical* question. In practice man must prove the truth, that is, the reality and power, the this-sidedness (*Diesseitigkeit*) of his thinking. The dispute over the reality or non-reality of thinking which is isolated from practice is a purely *scholastic* question.[26]

Marx promised to dissolve the "theoretical bubble-blowing" of German religion and philosophy by altering circumstances, not by further theoretical discussion.[27] Under Communism it is in the party that one discerns the locus of that wonderful instrument, Marxist-Leninist theory, which forms the basis for concrete action; Stalin's *History of the Communist Party of the Soviet Union* declares:

> The power of the Marxist-Leninist theory lies in the fact that it enables the Party to find the right orientation in any situation, to understand the inner connection of current events, to foresee their course and to perceive not only how and in what direction they are developing in the present, but how and in what direction they are bound to develop in the future.[28]

---

[25] *Mein Kampf*, p. 381.
[26] Karl Marx and Friedrich Engels, *op. cit.*, p. 243.
[27] "The German Ideology," *ibid.*, p. 260.
[28] *History of the Communist Party of the Soviet Union* (New York: International Publishers, 1939), p. 355. Quoted by Waldemar Gurian, *The Soviet Union* (Notre Dame, Ind.: Ave Maria Press, 1951), p. 1.

Events in Russian history demonstrate that before the realities of power ideological considerations must recede into the background. The ideology is destined to become the tool of those who have seized power. It is always couched in phrases broad enough to allow for *de facto* adaptions. Similarly, the institutions of society may function very effectively on their own local level while paying lip-service to the prevailing patterns of rationalization.

Still one has not fully understood or explained Communism or Nazism when he has shown that their claim to truth is void, that they do not adequately delineate conditions or aspects of reality which they claim to describe. Their effectiveness as bonds of community, within a nation or with neighboring nations, remains undeterred; certain common understandings animate the representatives of these ideologies; discussion is carried on against the background of commonly-accepted symbols, of *Mein Kampf,* or Marx's texts, or Mussolini's speeches. The symbolic and ritual use of the ideologies remains untouched by the most destructive argument.

7

IDEOLOGY AND THE QUESTION OF DEVOTION

> THE *Jacobin Revolution, which tried to institute*
> *the religion of virtue in order to establish unity*
> *upon it, will be followed by the cynical revolutions,*
> *which can be either of the right or of the left and*
> *which will try to achieve the unity of the world so*
> *as to found, at last, the religion of man. All that*
> *was God's will henceforth be rendered to Caesar.*
> ALBERT CAMUS, *The Rebel* (1951)

The term "ideology" encompasses the great political passions which locked in mortal combat during World War II. The term is commonly used to stand for almost any opinion or idea, for example, the "ideology of establishment," or the "ideology of Lutheranism." But more precise usage connects it with a system or body of ideas. The political passions have frequently been called "religions," and their tenets have been characterized as "national doctrines." They have also been called "secular nationalistic faiths," and their message has been understood as a "gospel."

Christianity, on the other hand, is frequently referred to as a "religious ideology" or as "Catholic ideology." It is understood to be an ideology competing with other, political ideologies, or it may be proclaimed the "supreme ideology." Again, it may be seen as "simply the most refined form of ideology." However, if these views are held with a recognition of the inescapable relativism and self-deception bound up with the term "ideology" it marks the total bankruptcy of Christian faith. From the perspective of Christian theology the pejorative aspects of the term render it highly questionable as a description of Christian faith. Its use in this connection supports the stand which sees all theology as "simple ideology."

The Threat to Ideology in Christian Commitment

Christian faith, on the contrary, remains a threat to the claims of every ideology. It introduces men to a realm of spiritual commitment and freedom which frees them from political bondage. Devotion to a kingdom not of this world forms a spiritual center for independent thought—and, possibly, for resistance. Under totalitarian regimes in which all labor unions, rival parties, and independent organizations have been dissolved the Christian church remains the sole center for effective opposition to exclusive claims. Though Karl Marx loved to upbraid religion, and Christianity in particular, as an ideological mask "covering up" the actual social situation, one must point unequivocally to a religious factor in the ideologies themselves. More than mere opinions are involved here. The questions about which the ideologies revolve—of origin, the nature of the universe, the nature of the historical process, man's destiny—are questions with which philosophy and religion have concerned themselves for millennia. They are questions regarding ultimates, and they elicit ultimate commitments. The ideologies form one aspect of this great quest. Logical positivists may say that these are finally meaningless questions, but as a matter of fact the majority of men continue to think and act in accordance with the answers they accept for these questions. Events in the last decade furnish conclusive proof that eminent scientists will betray their country because of ideological tenets. An ultimate devotion is given such world-views—a devotion which determines the basic direction of life. The six writers[1] of *The God That Failed* illustrate well the nature of Communist "faith." These writers could only be the more reluctant to surrender their convictions since they knew they could never again produce so total a commitment.

Here something in society, or society itself, in any case, some finite phenomenon, plays the role of the sacred. The sacred function is often betrayed by a tincture of theology in official language. A relentless ritual is often enacted in official pronouncements. The

[1] Richard Wright, Arthur Koestler, Ignazio Silone, André Gide, Stephen Spender, and Louis Fischer.

traditional language of religion has been repudiated and actual values may not even emerge explicitly, but some phenomena assume the role of the sacred. These are covert rather than overt religions. One may well hold that Nazism and Communism are merely pseudo-religions, on the basis that they involve no quest for what underlies reality.[2] However, if one's religion is defined as that to which one gives his ultimate devotion, on the basis of which ultimate decisions are made, then the Communist's devotion to the inveterate dialectic of history may be as "religious" as his former devotion to the Trinity. Notice the exclusion of "rival religions" in the "Statement by Erich Honecker Regarding Religion at the Thirty-fourth Plenary Session of the Central Committee of the Socialist Unity Party, February 3-6, 1958":

> The 34th Plenary Session of the Central Committee passed the resolution to arrange lectures, statements, and seminars on dialectical materialism in the Party organizations. Many Party organizations have already begun to put the resolution into effect.
>
> In this matter it is apparent that there are comrades who are of the opinion that one's world-view, particularly one's religion, is a private matter. The strength of the Marxist-Leninist Party of the working class, however, rests on the fact that the Party is actuated by a unified and closely-guarded scientific world-view which has no room for faith in a God, in supernatural powers, in superstition and reactionary ideas. It follows from this situation that the masses determine history, that the laws governing the development of nature, society, and thought can be known and be put to use for the realization of Socialism.
>
> In order that our Party may successfully fulfill its great historic task it is necessary that all members of the Party be made familiar with the world-view of Marxism-Leninism and that those comrades

---

[2] Within the limits of this study we cannot enter into the relationship, so important in all Continental discussion, between "man's religions" and "Christianity," or between the "sacred" and "religion." Although the writer prefers the definition of religion given here as the broader, generic concept, he acknowledges the significance of Becker's distinction: "It is therefore advisable to use sacred as the *general* term and religion and its equivalents as only *one* aspect thereof." Cf. Howard Becker and Harry Elmer Barnes, *Social Thought from Lore to Science* (2nd ed.; Washington, D. C.: Harren Press, 1952), Appendix iii, "1951 Commentary on Value System Terminology."

who still hold religious notions be helped by patient enlightenment to free themselves from the same.[3]

Here it is the march of dialectic through history, but for initiates into the Hitler Youth the Thousand Year Reich had the character of a sacred reality. According to a conventional approach to religion, or the theories of certain historians of religion, these devotions can only be considered as irreligious. But in their effort to give meaning to existence they evidence an orientation to something of ultimate and inclusive concern.[4]

The ideologies served to answer the emptiness and lack of direction of many who had been alienated from the Christian churches: they sought a faith in a cause which would at least transcend themselves. Although these people had lost their Christian convictions they continued their religious concerns. The human spirit requires ideas or ideals to spur on to meaningful endeavor. It requires meaning and purpose in life to take the place of its opposite, the sense of emptiness and indifference to all things. Fascism, Nazism, Democracy, Communism gave (and give) people this purpose. Hans Buchheim has shown how Hitler built a "political faith" on the basis of his resentful reflection on the meaning of human sacrifice, the cause of human misfortune, and the meaning of death:

> He sought to get at religious questions by means of political deliberations and to refer everything which in truth belongs to man's religion, namely, misfortune and sacrifice, human life and experience as a whole, to political values and political objectives. . . . The claim of the National Socialists that there had not been so much "believing" in Germany for many years as was to be found since 1933, or during the war years, is, indeed, not false; however, it was in every respect a degenerate belief, a belief false in content, intention, and mode.[5]

[3] Cited in *Vor der Jugendweihe die sozialistische Taufe.*

[4] Cf. Joachim Wach, *Types of Religious Experience* (Chicago: University of Chicago Press, 1951), pp. 32 ff. The national devotions are, according to Wach's criteria, pseudo-religious or semi-religious since they refer to some aspect of finite reality rather than to ultimate reality.

[5] Hans Buchheim, *Glaubenskrise im dritten Reich,* pp. 11, 17.

Karl Marx himself, who had said in his youth, "I hate all the gods," was animated by a religious devotion to vindicate the abused worker. Instead of fighting for the emancipation of Jews escaping the fetters of Europe's ghettos he embraced the cause of the depressed proletariat. Edmund Wilson has observed, "Nobody but a Jew could have fought so uncompromisingly and obstinately for the victory of the dispossessed classes."[6]

New Patterns of Integration

The process of disintegration has progressed so far that new principles and patterns of integration have replaced the Christian faith in Western nations. In one way or another, the Enlightenment dissolved the hold which religious convictions, customs, traditions—and bigotry—exercised on men's minds. It lifted scientific objectivity and political self-sufficiency to new levels of authority. It replaced Christian symbols with a new, secular set of symbols for which man himself was the organizing center and for which man's reasoning was the transforming tool: man was the source and center of the rights of man; no God needed to be invoked as their author or guarantor. Man had emancipated himself from old tyrannies, and in view of his firm position in nature these tyrannies might as well be supreme beings as feudal impediments. He had come to full age and must now assert his incontestable rights. The skepticism regarding Christian tenets which had spread so rapidly already in the seventeenth century emerged in the nihilism which Nietzsche recognized and sought to overcome.

When one enters into the question af the newness or uniqueness of the ideologies of recent centuries one must at least face the question how new or different they actually are. One could very well maintain that ideologies are no new thing on the intellectual or political horizon. One might understand Gnostic speculation and the Stoic system revolving about the universal rights of man and the fatherhood of God as ancient ideological forms. One

[6] Edmund Wilson, *To the Finland Station*, p. 307.

might interpret the politico-economic expectations of the Enthu-
siasts of the Reformation period or the eschatological hopes of
Joachim of Flora as ideologies, though Joachim's theories appear
to rise from a private rather than a social matrix. However, there
are senses in which the ideologies bear a closer resemblance to the
state religions of antiquity than to anything in more recent history.
Here, as in the ancient world, religion is considered a part of the
mores patrii and a distinctly national possession.[7] Both Nazism and
Fascism based their operations on the ancient maxim *salus populi
suprema lex.* The religions of antiquity did not claim universality;
they were understood to be the particular possession of a particular people or nation.

Christianity broke with the conception of religion as bound to
a state cult. It claimed universal significance for a particular Savior
and set out, by appealing to a strict personal commitment, to establish an international allegiance. It granted the duty of allegiance to the state, since, as St. Paul declared, the state had been
ordained by God as a good order of creation. The state is a good,
indeed, but a partial and particular good. It is not the *bonum
consummatum* worthy of the Christian's ultimate devotion. Christianity staunchly opposed every effort to absolutize the things of
Caesar; it had to demur when required to offer sacrifice before
Caesar's image; when asked to speak the easy *Kyrios Kaisar* and
curse Christ, Christians pronounced *Kyrios Iēsous.* In all of this
the Christian was not required to believe that the emperor was
divine; he was merely expected to go through the appropriate rite.

In all its conflicts during the Middle Ages the church could
assert the supreme claim of God on the human soul in contrast to
the claims of Holy Roman emperors. But in the modern world
political and economic systems have again sought to gain the individual's allegiance, and they have not added the concession "only
within certain limits."[8] All the feelings and sentiments which had

---

[7] Cf. George La Piana, "Theology of History," in J. R. Strayer (ed.), *The Interpretation of History* (New York: Peter Smith, 1950), p. 151.

[8] Cf. Eric Weil, "Religion and Politics," *Confluence,* IV, 2 (1955), 208.

earlier been attached to religion have been poured into the symbolism of the ideologies. In the case of their leading initiates the ideologies represent highly conscious forms of neo-paganism in contrast to the "unconscious paganism" of the early Christian era.

Spiritual Centers with a Vengeance

One of the factors in the present cultural situation which, in contrast to earlier centuries, has provided the setting for the ideologies is the ever-increasing trend toward the "mass man."[9] Neither ancient nor medieval man was engulfed in the masses. It is in connection with this development that one must understand certain features of the rites of the ideologies: new dogmas and rituals have been created to provide meaning and purpose for personal and social life. They reflect something of the numbering of man, a process which deprives man of his distinctive selfhood. Older institutions and values which had sustained previous generations have been dissolved by rapid social change and by the kind of radical criticism Nietzsche leveled against the sham religiosity of his day. Men were retaining a tenuous relationship to a church and community organization, but a vital faith was gone, along with the will to assume responsibility for the health of church and community.[10] Men had been loosed from the ties of family and friends, from older community values and ceremonies. They were left anxious and lonely amid new social forces, the concentration of economic power, and the demoralizing influence of meaningless labor. They wished freedom from the old constraints but dreaded the uncertainty of their unanswered questions. Hitler understood the weakness of the masses well; he stated:

Like the woman, whose psychic state is determined less by grounds

---

[9] Cf. Raymond Aron, *The Century of Total War,* pp. 143-144. Emile Durkheim describes modern men in a technical society which fails to give them rules to adhere to as the "anomic mass." Cf. *Suicide,* trans. John A. Spaulding and George Simpson, ed. with an introd. by George Simpson (Glencoe, Ill.: The Free Press, 1951), *passim.*

[10] See the discussion of the masses in Hannah Arendt, *The Origins of Totalitarianism,* pp. 301 ff. She points out how the modern masses reflect the experience of their "superfluity on an overcrowded earth" (pp. 430-31).

of abstract reason than by an indefinable emotional longing for a force which will complement her nature and who, consequently, would rather bow to a strong man than dominate a weakling, likewise the masses love a commander more than a petitioner and feel inwardly more satisfied by a doctrine, tolerating no other beside itself, than by the granting of liberalistic freedom with which, as a rule, they can do little, and are prone to feel that they have been abandoned. They are equally unaware of their shameless spiritual terrorization and the hideous abuse of their human freedom, for they absolutely fail to suspect the inner insanity of the whole doctrine.[11]

The totalitarian movements or the party itself became father and mother, son and daughter, to these isolated mass men. They were ready to give themselves to a cause, to another superior to themselves. The devotion furnished a new spiritual center. Yet, unlike the old spiritual center of Christian imprint, it required identical obedience, even identical facial expression of its adherents. Martin Bormann, executive head of the Nazi Party and liquidator of German Jews, was completely convinced of the irreconcilability of Nazism and the churches. Here is his statement on the "Relationship of National Socialism and Christianity":

> National Socialist and Christian concepts are irreconcilable. Christian churches build on uncertainty of human beings and attempt to preserve the uncertainty of as wide segments of the population as possible, for only in this way can Christian churches keep their power. As opposed to that, National Socialism is based on scientific fundamentals. Christianity has invariable tenets, which were set up almost 2,000 years ago and have crystalized in dogmas incompatible with reality. National Socialism on the other hand must, if it is to fulfill its job in the future, always be organized according to the latest knowledge of scientific research.
>
> Christian churches have always recognized the dangers which threaten their existence on account of exact scientific knowledge and therefore attempt by means of pseudo-science, such as theology is, to suppress or falsify scientific research by means of their dogma. Our National Socialist ideology is far loftier than the concepts of Chris-

[11] *Mein Kampf*, p. 42.

tianity, which in their essential points have been taken over from Jewry. For this reason also we do not need Christianity.

No human being would know anything of Christianity if it had not been drilled into him in his childhood by pastors. The so-called dear God in no wise gives knowledge of his existence to young people in advance but in an astonishing manner in spite of his omnipotence leaves this to the efforts of the pastors. If, therefore, in the future our youth learns nothing more of this Christianity, whose doctrines are far below ours, Christianity will disappear by itself.

It is also strange that before the beginning of today's calculation time (calendar) nothing was known of this Christian God and that also since this moment most inhabitants of the earth never learned anything of this Christianity and therefore according to the standard of Christian concept were damned from the beginning.

When we National Socialists speak of a belief in God, we do not understand by God, like naive Christians and their spiritual opportunists, a human-type being, who sits around somewhere in the sphere. We must rather open people's eyes to the fact that beside our small universe, highly important in the great universe, there are an inconceivably large number of other bodies in the universe, innumerable additional bodies, which like the sun are surrounded by planets, and these in turn by smaller bodies, the moons. The force of natural law, with which all these innumerable planets move in the universe, we call the Almighty or God. The claim that this world force is concerned about the fate of every single being, of every smallest earth bacillus, can be influenced by so-called prayers or other astonishing things, is based on a proper dose of naïveté or (however) on a business shamelessness.

As opposed to that, we National Socialists impose on ourselves the demand to live naturally as much as possible, i.e., biologically. The more accurately we recognize and observe the laws of nature and of life, the more we adhere to them, so much the more do we conform to the will of the Almighty. The more insight we have into the will of the Almighty the greater will be our successes.

It follows from the irreconcilability of National Socialist and Christian concepts, that a strengthening of existing confessions and every demand of originating Christian confessions is to be rejected by us. A differentiation between the various Christian confessions is not to be made here. For this reason also the thought of an erection of an evangelical National Church by merger of the various evangelical churches has been definitely given up, because the evangelical church is just as inimical to us as the Catholic Church. Any strengthening of the evangelical church would merely react against us.

It was a historical mistake of the German Emperors in the Middle Ages, that they repeatedly created order at the Vatican in Rome. It is always an error into which we Germans unfortunately fall too often, that we attempt to create order where we would needs have an interest in disunion and separation. The Hohenstaufens would needs have had the greatest interest in the disintegration of circumstances of Ecclesiastical power. From the standpoint of the Reich, it would have been most favorable if not one pope but at least two, if possible even more popes had existed and mutually fought. Instead of this the German emperors and especially the Hohenstaufens repeatedly looked after order in the church, helped one pope to power over all other rivals, with the success that the emperors, as soon as the pope was again strong enough for it, immediately received the first blows from "their" pope. The church, however, in strengthening its own position of power, repeatedly used the particularism of the princes and later of parties and tied it up with all its strength.

In former generations leadership of the people lay exclusively in the hands of the church. The state limited itself to issuing laws and orders and primarily to administering. The real leadership of the people lay not with the state but with the church. The latter exerted via the priest the strongest influence on the life of the individual human being, of families and on the totality (of things). Everything which did not suit the churches was suppressed with unprecedented ruthlessness. For centuries the state by the most various turns granted to the church the possibility of influence. It depended on the church, whether it would help the state or oppose it. The state was reduced to the aid of the church, it was dependent on it. The struggle of the German Emperors against the pope had to fail in the Middle Ages and repeatedly in modern times, because not the emperor, but the church had the leadership of the people in its hand.

This ideological dependence of the state on the church, the yielding of leadership of the people to the church, had become a matter of course, so that nobody dared to oppose seriously here. To consider this not as an incontrovertible fact from the beginning, passed as absurd stupidity until just before the *Machtübernahme* [Hitler's rise to power in 1933].

For the first time in German history the Führer consciously and completely has the leadership of the people in his own hand. With

156

the party, its components and attached units the Führer has created for himself, and thereby the German Reich leadership, an instrument which makes him independent of the church. All influences which might impair or damage the leadership of the people exercised by the Führer, with help of the NSDAP, must be eliminated. More and more the people must be separated from the churches and their organs, the pastors. Of course, the churches must and will, seen from their viewpoint, defend themselves against this loss of power. But never again must an influence on leadership of the people be yielded to the churches. This (influence) must be broken completely and finally.

Only the Reich government and by its direction the party, its components and attached units, have a right to leadership of the people. Just as the deleterious influences of astrologers, seers and other fakers are eliminated and suppressed by the state, so must the possibility of church influence also be totally removed. Not until this has happened does the state leadership have influence on the individual citizens. Not until then are people and Reich secure in their existence for all the future.

We would repeat the mistakes which in past centuries were fatal to the Reich, if we, according to the knowledge of our ideological opponents of the Christian confessions, were to contribute in any way to the strengthening of one of the various churches. The interest of the Reich lies not in conquering but in preserving and strengthening ecclesiastical particularism.

(signed) M. Bormann
Reichsleiter[12]

The erection of the National Socialist spiritual center can only be understood in its relation to the breakdown of the spiritual center which Christianity provided for the heart of Europe. Just as the cement of Roman religion was replaced by the new universalism of Christianity in the medieval, Christian empire, now new and more effective bonds were sought to provide social cohesion for disillusioned masses. The state in the totalitarian movements has not interpreted its task as one of promoting and adjudicating the common good but of itself being for its populace "the good" of all.

---

[12] This document was issued by Bormann in 1942 as a strictly confidential letter to the *Gauleitung. Nazi Conspiracy and Aggression,* VI, 1036-39.

THE QUESTIONS OF LOYALTY AND SOLIDARITY
8

> GOD *is weak and powerless in the world, and that is exactly the way, the only way, in which he can be with us and help us.*
>
> DIETRICH BONHOEFFER, *Letters and Papers from Prison* (1944)

The consecrations of the modern Caesars bring into clear focus the fact that traditional religions offer but one form of loyalty to compete for men's devotion. The cult of the ideologies indicates the final claim of conditioned loyalties. These loyalties have often been far more cogent than religious beliefs. Dostoyevsky saw that the Socialism of his day had assumed religious dimensions: "For Socialism is not merely the labour question, it is before all things the atheistic question, the question of the form taken by atheism today, the question of the tower of Babel built without God, not to mount to Heaven from earth but to set up Heaven on earth."[1]

The divine beings suffusing modern history have been the political communities; new things have been found sacred by modern man, things simply not available to ancient or medieval men. We have considered the loyalty involved in the rites of passage. Now let us consider the military oath sworn by recruits to the East German Peoples' Army:

I swear: at all times faithfully to serve the German Democratic Republic, my fatherland, and to defend it against every enemy upon orders of the Workers' and Farmers' Government.

I swear: by the side of the Soviet Army and the armies of the Socialist countries allied with us to be ready at all times to serve as a soldier of the National Peoples' Army, to defend Socialism against all enemies, and to stake my life for the winning of victory.

---

[1] *The Brothers Karamazov*, trans. Constance Garnett (New York: Modern Library, n.d.), p. 28.

I swear: to be an honorable, brave, disciplined, and alert soldier, to give unconditional obedience to military superiors, to obey orders with all decisiveness, and always carefully to preserve military and state secrets.

I swear: conscientiously to gain military knowledge, to abide by military regulations, and in every way to defend the honor of our Republic and its national Peoples' Army. Should I at any time violate this my festive oath may I encounter the severe punishment of the laws of our Republic and the contempt of our working people.[2]

The objective of this oath is the winning of unconditional loyalty to the regime. The unconditional obedience invoked here is something frightful to contemplate. The oath enlists a political allegiance to Socialism, in the sense of state and society, as well as to Socialism in the sense of an ideology, dialectical materialism—the atheistic undergirding for a socio-political superstructure. The compulsory military service law specifically appeals to the Ten Commandments of Socialist Morality. The opinion and authority of the Communist collective replaces the individual's conscience as final arbiter of conduct. And the recruit relinquishes any ground for appeal in case of question. In fact, he already proclaims his sentence!

What Is Your God?

The question is finally that of one's ultimate loyalty: What is your God? In his explanation of the First Commandment Martin Luther stated the alternatives in classical terms:

What is it to have a god? What is God? Answer: A god is that to which we look for all good and in which we find refuge in every time of need. To have a god is nothing else than to trust and believe him with our whole heart. As I have often said, the trust and faith of the heart alone make both God and an idol. If your faith and trust are right, then your God is the true God. On the other hand, if your trust is false and wrong, then you have not the true God.

[2] "Zum sowjetzonalen Wehrpflichtgesetz," *Herder-Korrespondenz,* XVI, 8 (May, 1962), 380.

For these two belong together, faith and God. That to which your heart clings and entrusts itself is, I say, really your God.[3]

While emphasizing the inescapable positive values of man's social and political activity, the Christian faith always returns to the relative rather than the absolute significance of nation, people, or social aspirations. It will point to the provisional character even of man's noblest achievements, to the ambiguities of his most illustrious social experiments. The God who works dynamically in history is the God beyond all gods. There is power in the gods of nations and of social programs; there is partial participation here in that "power of being" by which all things have being. St. Augustine expressed this thought already when he spoke of the gods of the earthly city: "For created gods are gods not by virtue of what is in themselves, but by a participation of the true God."[4] In the same spirit Luther could characterize the monks of his day as *fabricatores deorum,* as men who had formed God in their own image.[5]

Thus one of the resources Christianity possesses in the face of the ideologies is its ability to criticize all religious devotions in the name of the supreme God. For example, the Life and Work Conference at Oxford in 1937 could declare that the idea of unlimited national sovereignty was irreconcilable with the lordship of Jesus Christ. The death of Jesus Christ stands in judgment over every merely human determination of the good. Allegiance to the self, to race, to the state, to particular forms of church polity, are seen before the cross to include pitiful distortions of the good. The truly Good, the One who does the will of God, is crucified, and the plans of wicked men triumph on the plains of human history.

The existence and stand of a strong church and strong churchmen have been among the strongest bulwarks against the ideologies. Although the performance of the great mass of church mem-

---

[3] *The Large Catechism of Martin Luther,* trans. Robert H. Fischer (Philadelphia: Muhlenberg Press, 1959), p. 9.
[4] *The City of God,* Bk. XIV, Chap. 13 (p. 461 in the Modern Library ed.).
[5] "Ionas propheta," *Weimar Ausgabe,* XIII, 229, ll. 11-12.

bers under Hitler was anything but admirable, especially with respect to the persecution of the Jews, there was a "remnant" that stood up and was counted. Albert Einstein was led to praise the determination of the Christian churches to defend truth and freedom when their old defenders, the universities and newspapers, had been silenced within a few weeks.[6] Religious and non-religious humanists showed themselves entirely unable to maintain their autonomous centers of opposition against this new heteronomy. Yet one cannot establish, by means of inference from the inadequacies of these secular alternatives, the truth or credibility of the Christian faith. Faith remains a devotion to and obedience to one's personally present Lord. It may find support and gain some partial clarification of its nature through an examination of abortive efforts to solve the problems of the community and individual. But since faith involves a personal relationship, rather than a relation to some object or set of ideas, its adventurous quality of trust in an "unknown, untried, unfelt goodness" must defy all efforts to "establish" its truth.

In What Do You Participate?

The great positive thrust of these "political churches" in the direction of solidarity and creative achievement is, again, a necessary though distorted value. Both Nazism and Communism have presented themselves as brotherhoods, participation in which will necessarily unleash creative energies. National Socialism interpreted the party as a vast comradeship, so that the "German greeting," "Heil Hitler," is to be understood against the background of this essential brotherhood. Nazism showed itself to be a community of "One Fold and One Shepherd," after the model of the Christian church. This brotherhood is illustrated in the trial of Father Max Metzger, martyred leader of the Una Sancta Brotherhood, before the Peoples' Court in Berlin. In the course of the trial President Dr. Roland Freisler asked Metzger, "What is this

[6] *Time,* December 23, 1940, p. 38.

Una Sancta?" Metzger quietly began to explain, "Christ has founded only one church . . . ." But at this point Freisler broke in, "Una Sancta! Una Sancta! . . . Una! Una! We are that! And there isn't any other!"[7]

The Communist Party has provided authority and purpose for many alienated souls. It has endeavored to overcome man's isolation from his neighbor; it has sought to restore to integral communities individuals who have lost their identity in rootless crowds. The final goal appears to be a kind of "state church of atheism." For neither Nazism or Communism is there anything beyond corporate society which deserves one's allegiance. For Christian faith, on the other hand, true participation in the reconstruction of society must always follow upon participation in the Body of Christ. And such participation is no simple possibility for man's creative endeavors, but may be gained only when the "middle wall of separation" from God has been broken down, when the hostility and wrath occasioned by sin have been overcome by the cross of Christ and one is incorporated into the new household of God (Eph. 2:11 ff.). The brotherhood offered by these political loyalties must be answered in the same way Tertullian answered the washings and banquetings of paganism in his day: "All your washings point to the need for baptism and all your banquetings to the need for eucharist."

Totalitarian regimes tend to consider the role of the church in terms of its liturgical services: scheduled Sunday services and liturgical rites are permitted to continue without interference. The relegation of the role of the church to a sort of "souls-in-heaven" spirituality must be seen as a crippling limitation on its full task, but one must recognize that such a situation cannot fully destroy its effectiveness. It may be a positive strength if, as demonstrated under Nazi and Communist control, worship once more forms the center and pulsebeat of the Christian life. One of the positive results of the church struggles has been a new and vital recognition

[7] Cf. Leonard Swidler, "Max Josef Metzger: Witness for Peace and Unity," *American Benedictine Review*, XIII (1962), 153-86.

of the role of worship in community within the Christian life.

Christian worship does not revolve about "cunningly devised fables" or impressive pageantry. It is essentially a re-living, a re-presentation of the events of God's dealing with his people in history, particularly in the life of God's Son. It is not governed by emotional or aesthetic or symbolic considerations and it is not concerned with abstract ideas. It is God's present action, through his Word and Sacrament, re-enacting, as the year of the church unfolds, the once-and-for-all action of God in dealing with Old and New Israel. It presents justification by grace through faith, whereby the believer enjoys peace with God rather than a life under his wrath. It sends the believer out into the world under the power of the Spirit to heal and reunite relations which are fractured and bent.

The God of Christian worship is the Lord of history. He is beyond national—including American—manageability. Christian faith sees him as guiding events in history according to his purposes, judging, healing, and renewing the earth. As such, Christian faith guards against an easy optimism which insists that everything must come out well for America and it guards against a pessimism which despairs of the future. God, who "judges the heart," will use even the evil of sinful men to accomplish his purposes.

Within Christian worship one may hope that the full dynamic power of God's law as well as of the Gospel may hold sway. American churches today are presenting a Christianity without law, a vitiated and distorted version of Christian faith. Theological integrity and restored discipline would involve setting forth the convicting, condemning message of God's law in all its disturbing, destroying power—before the life-giving message of the Gospel that raises up sin-bruised hearts is proclaimed.

However, one cannot acquiesce in any attempt to reduce Christianity to cultic and ascetical matters. To a considerable degree, the neglect of social problems by the German churches had paved the way for the phenomenal success of the ideologies. In Germany between the wars both the industrial workers and the cultured classes had become alienated from Christianity.[8] The Christian faith requires that the life of obedience under the Word, lived by the power of the Holy Spirit, and the social consequences of Christian teaching be kept intimately united. In the face of the strongest opposition the commitment of Christian faith must pass from confessions and liturgical forms to social expression. Karl Marx's pointed charge that all previous philosophers have merely *interpreted* the world whereas the essential task remains to *change* it has not been acknowledged by the Christian churches in all its unmasking power. Modern Socialism's interest in social justice has not called forth among Christians the determined rethinking and rebuilding required to annul this one, bitter charge. If God is involved in the "depths" of human life as creator and continuous renewer, then he desires a people who will witness and act for justice. If God is really at work through the Gospel, reclaiming people for his work in the world, then these people are to be open with a new receptivity to the Holy Spirit who inspires them to go forth into the world.

Moreover, in order to become a *living church* the Christian community must draw its members into a united and committed body about the Word and Sacraments. The significance of the Christian sacraments is illustrated by the fact that in Russia, after several generations of atheistic pressures, Russian clergy claim that approximately fifty per cent of all Russian children are still baptized. The church ought also to be ready to learn from its opponents: as an institution it should compare in compactness, indoctrination, and efficiency with the Communist cells which have worked against it. Cultural forms and social structures once considered indispensable may have to give way to patterns in closer harmony with the Gospel.[9] In East Germany the office of elder has

---

[8] Cf. James Hastings Nichols, *History of Christianity, 1650-1950* (New York: Ronald Press, 1956), pp. 384-85.

[9] Note the present rethinking, in this country and abroad, of the doctrine and practice of confirmation. See e.g., Lukas Vischer, *Die Geschichte der Konfirmation* (Zollikon: Evangelischer Verlag, 1958), pp. 105-114; also *Confirmation: History, Doctrine, and Practice*, ed. Kendig Brubaker Cully (Greenwich, Conn.:

been revamped. It has come to be understood as involving spiritual service not only within the congregation but also "outside," in the factory, on collective farms, and in hospitals. The elders are true "actives," to use a favorite Communist term. They represent their distinctive understanding of life in the complex circles of an alien society. It is thus no coincidence that in the intercessory prayers offered there the majority of names of those imprisoned are those of laymen rather than pastors.[10]

Christians today must be ready to slough off whatever is peripheral in their faith so that they may base their thinking and living on the solid foundations once established by Christ and the apostles, learning to live, once again, by the faith that the direction of events in history does not emerge from history but is given to history by its Lord. Such faith should open the eyes of the Christian to the blandishments of the second beast of the Apocalypse, the beast which rises from the earth and is identified with the false prophet. As described in the thirteenth chapter of Revelation, this second beast exercises all the power of the first: it causes the inhabitants of the earth to worship the first beast, the totalitarian state. The second beast is the religious propaganda power of the totalitarian state.[11] By the wonders it accomplishes it deceives the inhabitants of the earth. The Roman state already laid claim to a devotion which the Christian must reserve for God alone; it laid claim to being a redemptive society which exercised powers over and conferred graces upon its subjects. If this can be said of the Roman

Seabury Press, 1962); and Arthur C. Repp, *Confirmation in the Lutheran Church* (St. Louis: Concordia, 1964). The Roman Catholic rethinking of confirmation appears to have led more clearly in the direction of an active lay apostolate, toward a courageous and empowered lay priesthood, than have Protestant efforts. Cf. J. A. Jungmann, *Handing on the Faith: A Manual of Catechetics,* trans. A. N. Fuerst (New York: Herder and Herder, 1959). Of the many books on the reshaping of congregational forms and structures, cf. e.g., George Webber, *The Congregation in Mission* (New York: Abingdon, 1964), and Martin E. Marty *et al., Death and Birth of the Parish* (St. Louis: Concordia, 1964).

[10] *Evangelisches Gemeindeblatt Ulm,* April 1, 1962, p. 11.

[11] Cf. Oscar Cullman, *The State in the New Testament* (New York: Charles Scribner, 1956), pp. 76-78.

state it can be said with equal certainty of many political appeals today.

Wanted: A Courageous, Confessing Church

Yet when all these things have been said, one should add that the most important lesson the churches may have to learn is the steadfast willingness to suffer in the face of persecution in the totalitarian state. Judged by human standards, the situation of the church in the East Zone of Germany appears to be hopeless. A new dark age appears to be descending. The means at the disposal of the state are so vast, the faith and practice of the newly emancipated churches so wavering that the outcome of the struggle seems to present no doubts. Struggles of allegiance and of conscience as well as heroic, suffering faith become evident each day. So vast and continuous are the means that the modern state has at its disposal that those under obedience to a kingdom not of this world find themselves powerless and alone; they can hope for no spectacular vindication of the Christian Gospel or the Christian understanding of life, but must rely on Christian hope, on patience, and prayer under affliction. They are engaged in a continual, invisible struggle. One is reminded of Pastor Martin Niemoeller's admonition in his last sermon before imprisonment:

> Now we are fighting for the cross, for faith or unbelief, for the sovereignty of the crucified Christ or the sovereignty of the prince of this world. And we must not dream of peace, indeed we must not even hope for a truce, but we must clearly realize that we are being called upon to make a last bid for victory by the message of the Cross, which saves us from the power of the world and its prince and gives us the peace of God, so that we may not perish in this final battle, with its more than human temptations.

> Possibly the world can bear individual Christians, possibly it can tolerate the principle that each individual must be saved in his own way; but, as long as it wants to be itself, it cannot seriously want the Church of the Cross, but must fight against it one way or another; and the more determinedly the world approves of itself, the more sharply must it resist a message which is based upon the belief that

this world must pass away, nay more, that the judgment of God has already been pronounced upon it.[12]

Thus events of the last several decades have called forth a faith which is virile because it is rooted in the abiding Word and Sacraments, joyous because it foresees victory "through him who loves us." A renewed seriousness, more vital worship, a new dedication on the part of Christians to Christian teaching and ethical norms, a quickened sensitivity to ultimate claims and demands made in the name of less than ultimate systems or political orders, an increased awareness of the social consequences of the Christian faith and a willingness to engage in social and political action, identification through sharing (if only in token form), fervent prayer for Christian brethren under affliction—these remain the answer of Christians to the ideologies. In recent decades a new kind of church has been emerging in the face of opposition, a confessing church. Sacrifices comparable to those which Communists are willing to make have again become incumbent on Christians—also on privileged American Christians. The ideologies have perceived and have caricatured much that is false in traditional Christian customs and practices, but they have revealed the whole distance between Christian faith and political surrogates. The consecrations of Caesar reveal with particular clarity the relevance of Bishop Dibelius' statement for each of us: "We are living in an hour of grave decisions. But then it is not only a grave hour. It is also the hour of opportunities with an infinite greatness."[13]

[12] Quoted by Franklin H. Littell in *The Free Church* (Boston: Beacon Press, 1957), p. 91, from Martin Niemoeller, *First Commandment* (London: Wm. Hodge and Co., 1937), p. 238.

[13] *Report to the Evangelical Church in Germany,* p. 17.

APPENDICES

LIST OF NAZI PERIODICALS AND MANUALS

Die Feier: Schrift für Lebensführung und Feiergestaltung in der SS. (1st issue, 1935?; 2nd issue, 1943). "Published by the Reichsführer of the SS and the Chief of the Central Office of the SS. Intended for use only in the SS. Orders cannot be accepted."

Die Gestaltung der Lebensfeiern (Berlin, 1942). "Published by the Führer's Deputy for the supervision of the entire spiritual and ideological schooling and education of the NSDAP. Guidelines. For use only in the services."

Idee und Tat. "Instructional material for the entire ideological development of the NSDAP. Published by the Office of the Führer's Deputy for the supervision of the entire spiritual and ideological schooling and education of the NSDAP. Issued as needed."

Informationsdienst (Berlin). "Issued by The Youth Office of the Reich. Appears monthly. Responsible: Bannführer Werner Kley. Confidential! For use only in the inner service."

Die neue Gemeinschaft. (A periodical published by the Central Cultural Office of the Propaganda Ministry giving guidelines for the planning and execution of Nazi festivals and for the use of leisure time.)

Organisationsbuch der NSDAP. (Edited by Dr. Robert Ley, the Reichsorganisationsleiter of the Nationalsozialistische Deutsche Arbeiterpartei, i.e. the Nazi Party. Munich: Franz Eher, 1938.)

SA-Mann. (Organ of the Nazi Storm Troopers.)

Schwarzes Korps. (Weekly published by the SS.)

Völkischer Beobachter. (Munich newspaper which became the official Nazi Party organ; Alfred Rosenberg was the chief editor.)

BASIC CONSIDERATIONS IN THE PLANNING AND EXECUTION OF SOCIALIST CEREMONIES IN CONNECTION WITH BIRTHS, MARRIAGES, AND DEATHS IN STALINSTADT[1]

I. *Basic Considerations*

1. Birth, union of man and woman, and death were originally biological processes, which, however, in virtue of man's development have gained great social significance.

The exploiting classes have given these events idealistic, religious significance and churchly ceremonial forms in order to bind the people to themselves and subject them to their own rule.

In recent times the suppressed classes have defended themselves, and continue to defend themselves, against interpretations alien to life; they are looking for secular forms to mark these outstanding events in human life.

The workers' class of the German Democratic Republic and its leading party begin with the dialectic-materialist world-view and, with the help of the Socialist state, seek to mark birth, marriage, and death ceremonially as events of life in the nascent Socialist society.

2. The content of these workers' ceremonies is Socialist humanism, which is atheistic and recognizes no higher being than the humanity which is working and struggling for peace, democracy, and socialism.

Socialistic humanism rouses the pride of the workers in their world-revolutionary creative power and stimulates the workers, led by the working class and its Marxist-Leninist Party, in harmony with the laws of nature and society, to free all men from exploitation and suppression, to establish the equitable Socialistic and finally the Communistic order of society, which will abound in material as well as spiritual goods.

---

[1] Now renamed Eisenhüttenstadt, Stalinstadt, like Nowa Huta, in Poland, is understood to be a symbol of the new Socialist society. The provisions here outlined are therefore especially significant. City planning in Stalinstadt and Nowa Huta originally made no provisions for churches.

The content of these ceremonies results from linking the individual experiences and efforts of parents, bridal couples, and survivors to the progressive endeavors of man. These celebrations will be replete with meaning if individual aspirations are found to harmonize with the general goals.

3. In the transitional periods between capitalism and socialism the coincidence of personal and social interests cannot always be assumed in individual instances. In fact, there are usually such contradictions operative in the [social] consciousness of individuals that these contradictions must necessarily be uncovered and set aside.

For that reason, in approaching the work of preparing for and celebrating the ceremonies connected with birth, marriage, and death, the Socialist state has the task of bringing Socialist educational influences to bear upon parents, engaged couples, and the bereaved. This educational task is most important in the realm of the planning and execution of public ceremonies occasioned by events in the life of the individual.

II. *Organization*

1. The City Council of Stalinstadt passed a resolution giving expression to the basic considerations stated above, and it created a planning office to see to the development and carrying out of Socialistic ceremonies to be conducted at birth, marriage, and death.

The official in charge of this office bears complete responsibility for the preparation and execution of these ceremonies. He conducts the preliminary conversations, directs the organizational and technical details, and gives the addresses. To identify this colleague for the public the designation "Speaker of the City Council" was created. Designations like "Dedication Speaker" or "Orator" were found unacceptable.

2. Originally it was planned that the Speaker would be given a post in the Division of Inner Affairs, the Registrar's Office. This plan was dropped, however, in order to free the Speaker from the legal and documentary tasks of the Registrar's Office. In order to accent the cultural and educational task of the Speaker he was placed under the head of the Division of Culture.

In practice, however, the speaker stands closer to the Registrar's Office than to the Division of Culture. He shares the public office hours of the Registrar's Office, is provided there with pertinent information, and celebrates the ceremonies held in conjunction with the educational and marriage vows in the wedding room.

He speaks there, in the place of the Commissioner of the Office of Vital Statistics, at every wedding, also in cases where no provision is made for the wedding vow. The authorization for this procedure was strengthened inasmuch as the Council decided to name the Speaker "Representative of the Commissioner of the Office of Vital Statistics."

In accordance with these considerations the City Council's allocations were extended to cover the following:

a) Equipment of the Festive Room (wedding room) with musical instruments, plants, etc.

b) The speaker's salary, in accordance with Group II VBV.

c) Production of the texts for the vow; production of the documents.

d) Gifts of flowers to the parents and bridal couple.

III. *Conversations*

1. The preparations for the ceremonies provide for basic conversations with parents, the engaged pair, and survivors. Already in these conversations, and especially here, the cultural and educational function of the workers' and farmers' state will be exercised. No ceremonies may be conducted unless such clarifying discussions have taken place.

The methodology of these conversations must be that of Marxist-Leninist convictions, with their firmly grasped principles and their patience. This methodology always embraces the speaker's taking the offensive and the guarantee of freedom of decision for those with whom he is engaged in discussion.

2. The first goal of these discussions is the establishing of a personal acquaintance between the speaker and the main figures of the ceremonies being arranged. A relationship of confidence should emerge. The speaker must learn their background, the occupations they are engaged in, where and in what manner they are active—he must become acquainted with their social and intellectual outlook.

The second goal of these discussions is the clarification of principles underlying the various ceremonies.

The basic considerations spoken of in Part I should be clarified as follows:

a) The celebration of the birth of a child and of its Name Giving brings about the conscious alliance of the parents with the aspirations for the future of the entire productive people; it is the festive induction of the child into human society. For the child's sake the parents make a vow for its Socialist education.

b) The festive form of the wedding at the Registrar's Office imparts to the assent of man and wife the content of the Socialist ethic. For this reason the couple takes a Socialist wedding vow. Like the education vow, the ceremony is to be a public matter, in order to emphasize the social significance of this personal event.

c) The festive burial has as its content the noting of the good aspirations and deeds of the deceased. The proud satisfaction of having been bound to this man should comfort the mourners. The death of this man must encourage the survivors energetically to close the broken ranks.

The third goal of these discussions is agreement regarding the particulars of these ceremonies, i.e., regarding the participation of the relatives and the public, regarding the vow, regarding the musical portions and associated technical questions.

IV. *Vows*

1. The Socialist education vow may take the following form (if the child's mother is married):

Vow: "Before forward-striving humanity, we, Emmi and Kurt Eisermann, responsible for ourselves and for our child, declare our marriage to be the indissoluble home for our son Jörg Eisermann, born on November 8, 1957, in Stalinstadt. Following the motto 'It depends on you, on all of us!' we vow to rear our son to be a Socialistically perceptive, thinking, and acting citizen of the German Democratic Republic."

Stalinstadt, _____ _____ _____

(date)   (mother's signature)   (father's signature)

2. In the case of a child born out of wedlock this vow may begin in the following manner:

Vow: "Before . . . etc., . . . I, Gisela Merten, responsible for my son, vow to be at all times a faithful mother. I vow, etc." Finally only the mother's signature.

3. The vow may, in addition, bear the signature of the sponsors. In such cases the parents' signatures may be supplemented somewhat as follows: "In order to help fulfill this vow we vow as sponsors. . . ."

4. The Socialist marriage vow may take the following form:

Vow: "Before all working people we, Gerda and Herbert Fischer, responsible for each other and for ourselves, vow to regard our marriage contracted here this day in mutual love as a fellowship for the whole of life. We vow to the workers' society to strengthen, by our common creative efforts, the Socialist achievements and the political power of workers and farmers. To one another we vow attentive esteem, thoughtfulness, help in time of need, mutual encouragement for vocational and cultural development, mutual decisions, and indissoluble faithfulness."

Place, date, signatures.

5. After the vows have been signed, they will be kept and filed. Following the profession of the vows, the married couple or the parents of the child receive a document which reproduces the text of the vow as a record, thus: "They vowed the workers. . . ." The document will be prepared on a folded sheet bearing on the outside the state coat of arms of the German Democratic Republic and within, beneath the text, the signature of the mayor and his seal. The printing of document forms was rejected, in order not to erase individual interest in our Socialist state. Therefore every document will be lettered by hand.

The House for Organizational Supplies (Berlin 0 34, Warschauer Strasse 60) supplies document sheets bearing the state coat of arms.

V. *Addresses*

1. To serve as the conclusion of the preliminary discussions the [ceremonial] address was devised. In the address the characteristic particulars of the life and thought of the parents, the bridal couple, or the deceased are linked to the struggle for freedom and the Socialist ideas of the workers so as to form a well-coordinated whole. The addresses in the Festival Room of the City Council point ahead to the vows. The address at the burial service is held before the casket is lowered into the earth. After the lowering of the casket only a few closing words follow, a very short speech in honor of the deceased and in exhortation of the survivors.

2. The basic outline of the address to parents is as follows:

a) The workers and farmers of the German Democratic Republic greet with joy each newborn child, since through their possession of political power and industrial strength they can promise each child a good future.

b) This future is Socialistic, and at the prime of life of today's infants it will be Communistic. Socialism and Communism are worthy of the common efforts of workers and of each individual, since only in such a society can man be permanently happy. The way to such a society will be prepared by the work, struggle, and power of the workers.

c) The ability to traverse this path is made possible by Socialist education. The first school is the family, which is to teach, in the solidity of marriage and in the reciprocal fulfillment of duties between parents and children, how one is to live in community. Succeeding schools will, together with the family, give the child a Socialist education: society with state educational centers, mass organizations, industries, etc.

d) As the children grow up, they require protection. The workers' and farmers' state guarantees and furnishes peace and freedom to workers. Together with the state the parents protect their children from external and internal perils. Religious protection fails here!

e) The parents and their friends (who may be sponsors) are called upon to confess their obligations over against humanity and the newborn child, to affirm and to sign the Socialist education vow.

3. The basic outline of the address to bridal couples:

a) The workers of the German Democratic Republic welcome the marriage vows of such people, since marriage in the German Democratic Republic enjoys a promising future and contributes to the Socialist ordering of human relations.

b) We acknowledge with joy this-worldly happiness. Beyond this life, outside the Socialist world, no one can enjoy happiness. Our happiness grows when we work together as respected personalities in the life of the people (Faust). It grows in Socialist endeavors and Socialist families.

c) We warn against the bourgeois conception of marriage. Exploitation as the basis for marriage leads to unfaithfulness in the man and corruption of character in the woman. To submit to exploitation leads to misery in the man and to degradation of the wife.

Under capitalism Socialist marriages were marked by their partnership in suffering and struggle. Through common social action Socialist marriages in the German Democratic Republic promote the joint happiness of the married couple.

d) Religion fails as a protection for marriage because of the impotence of the churches, because of the non-existence of God, and because of the churches' disregard for earthly life, as well as because of the immorality of those church leaders who approve of war as God's means for ruling the world and who set woman in subordination to man.—Socialist society protects and fosters marriage through legislation, the administration of justice on the part of the workers' and farmers' state, and through the morality of the workers, who fight for peace and social justice.

e) The married couple is called upon to do that which will do the most to provide permanent happiness, namely, to espouse the Socialist marriage vow, to sign it, and to conduct their lives according to it.

4. The basic outline of the address to survivors:

a) The death of a citizen in the German Democratic Republic is a painful loss to all farmers and workers; for we treasure every person as a part of our strength in the building of Socialism (this includes also adolescent and veteran workers, as bearers [respectively] of the future and of our good tradition).

b) We survey respectfully the life which has just come to an end and stress the energy with which the deceased has struggled. In so doing we condemn the exploiters, the militarists, the Fascists, who misuse human life.

c) We note the good the deceased has accomplished in the family, among his co-workers, and for friends in social organizations. We laud what he has created in work and social activity in the way of material and spiritual values, which he bequeaths, as a nameless monument, to the peoples' possession and consciousness.

d) We mark the breach which has arisen where he worked, in social functions, and in the family, and we voice our grief at the loss of this person.

e) We invite others to honor the deceased in that we propose, according to the strength given us, to close the breaches which have arisen, in order that the good intentions of the deceased may be realized. The image and example which the deceased has left in our memory should incite us to these ends.

f) It is our duty to commit the deceased to the earth so that, in keeping with his intentions, we may be able to foster further the improvement of life.

VI. *Participation of the Public*

1. Because of the social importance of the ceremonies it is important that large numbers of people participate in them. The ceremonies must be held, so far as possible, on days and at hours favorable to full attendance on the part of relatives, co-workers, organizations, housing cooperatives, etc.

The most appropriate time for the educational vows is Sunday morning.

2. In connection with the rendering of the educational vows and

the marriage vows persons closely concerned may take part as sponsors or witnesses and may also sign the respective certificates.

3. Participation on the part of the public should not be merely spontaneous. It should be organized with the help of the press and especially through the mass organizations. It is desirable that the National Front become the organizer of public participation. The initiative in each case must, however, come from the state apparatus.

VII. *The Ceremonies*

1. The ceremonies should, wherever possible, be accompanied throughout by music in order to bring out the special nature of the situation and to prepare the way for receiving the deep impression of the proceedings and addresses. The fee for the musician or musicians should be paid by the individuals themselves so that they will not regard these festive occasions passively and so they will not view these festivals simply as a gift from the state but as a Socialist endeavor undertaken mutually by state and individuals.

2. In the celebration of the educational vow music cannot be dispensed with. Following a brief greeting to the parents, the children, relatives, and other guests, the ceremony begins with festive music. The address then follows. After the address a short musical piece is played which prepares the way for the grave and significant questions involved in the educational vow. After the vow has been given, the child's mother, father, and the sponsors (if any) are invited in turn to add their signatures. The signing is to be carried out against an unbroken musical background. The music swells and stretches out over the act of affixing signatures. Following this the documents are read aloud, after which time they are handed to the child's parents.

Gifts and congratulations follow. A final festive musical selection in march time is played as the participants in the event leave the room. It should resound until people have passed beyond hearing distance.

3. The celebration of the marriage vow forms a unity with the joining in marriage at the Registrar's Office. The ceremony begins with a word of greeting from the Commissioner for Vital Statistics. Suitable music then follows. Then, in question and answer, the marriage is joined. The Commissioner affixes his signature to the marriage booklet. Thereupon the Speaker proceeds to the exchanging of the rings. Music then begins and leads into the address. After the address and affirmation of the marriage vow festive music is again played. Now

the Commissioner for Vital Statistics reads the marriage booklet aloud to ascertain its accuracy. He asks the parties to sign the booklet and the vow. During the signing and through the remainder of the ceremony music is played. Thereupon the Commissioner congratulates the couple and hands them the genealogical register and credentials; the Speaker then transmits, with his greeting, the document certifying the marriage vow. Parents and close relatives convey their congratulations as do delegates from the factory and the organizations. The music intones a festive march, which—with variations of the theme— accompanies the festive company as it leaves the room.

4. Burial rites are to be patterned after the well-known traditions of the workers' movement.[2]

[2] From *Kirchliches Jahrbuch* (1958), pp. 176-81.

EXAMPLE OF A WORSHIP SERVICE
OF THE GERMAN CHRISTIANS

(First Sketch)

"Bravery"

Organ Prelude

Hymn by the Congregation:

Tune: "Valet will ich dir geben"
Rise, people free and holy, bright dawns for you the day!
For from you now is taken all slavery, grief, and shame.
Rise up to deeds afresh, ye folk, in God's own time;
Within your heart will flower the strength of endless time.

Word of Entrance:

Thou giv'st the day, thou giv'st the night.
We stand, O God, within thy might.

Lord, give us also peace!
When earth and heaven reel and fall,
Lord, give us then a bright, new world!

We know that we and our times are in God's hand. Therefore we
confidently enter the day and sing the Creator's glory!

Hymn by the Congregation:

Tune: Its own tune, Hymn 17, or: "Nun freut euch, lieben
Christen gemein"
Oh, let us free and joyful be, the night is now full ended.
The day with its bright glow is here, our souls are made resplendent.
We gladly stand in this bright world; 'tis God who placed us in
    his light.
His grace and goodness shroud us.

O God, take thou our entire strength, soul, body, blood, and life!
He's done his day's work faithfully who thee his heart has given.
The painful toil turns brightest joy, a song of praise the evening bell.
To thee, O God, the glory.

SEARCHING OF THE HEART

The Congregation rises

The Threefold Thanksgiving:

Pastor:

Almighty, thou willst that the people live, that the individual mature
and prove himself. Therefore thou lovest the courage of those who
struggle and suffer, who offer themselves and die for Honor,
Freedom, and Fatherland.
Lord, thou blessest the good fight!

Congregation:

Lord God, we thank thee.

Pastor:

Thou showest the brave the way to light in the night,
   to peace in the midst of misery.
Lord, to faith thou givest victory!

Congregation:

Lord God, we thank thee.

Pastor:

Thou dost call us, the free, into thy holy kingdom *{Reich}*.
Therefore thou givest us strength for battle in our breast and in our
conscience against sin and guilt, against servitude and death.
Lord, thy grace giveth eternal life!

Congregation:

Lord God, we praise thee, we praise thee everlastingly.

The Congregation is seated

APPENDICES

The Word of Faith:

> Live fearlessly! Have confidence! Look up to him
> who sits in power. He guideth all things well.
>
> You can do but one thing: stand in your place without fear, employ
> your strength for the holiest objects, live and die in such service
> without wavering.
> So will you be brave and your life will be lucid.
> Everything beyond this is God's business.
>
> But know this: The most shameful thing is a
> servile mentality. God lives only in the proud heart;
> for the base mind heaven is too high.

(E. M. Arndt)

Response of the Congregation:

> Tune: "Valet will ich dir geben"
> We believe in and we trust in our Lord and Helper God,
> Who lets us view the sunshine, saves us from need and night.
> We stand with feet well-grounded, on this the earth of God,
> Who lit the starry heavens, yet holds our lives most dear.

PROCLAMATION

The Word of Eternal Truth:

> Be strong in the Lord and in the power of his might. Put on the
> armor of God, that you may stand fast against the wiles of the devil.
> Be vigilant, stand in faith, be manly and be strong!

Hymn by the Congregation:

> We trust in God and in his power, who has the world established.
> The Father watches anxiously, with him we stand united.
> He faithful stands here by our side, through every evil will abide.
> He gives us bread and strength for work. His tireless will all things
> creates.
>
> We faithful stand to Christian brethren, in stillness and in storm.
> The soul to battle has been called, this is the Father's willing.
> The flames of pure love cement us to our folk together.
> Such faith and honor unto death, they strengthen us, our Lord and
> God.

Sermon.

> The valiant face foes,
> Obedient unto death.
> The loftiest valor flows
> From thee, our Lord and God.

> It is a precious thing when the heart remains firm—
> that is a gift of grace.

Hymn by the Congregation: Hymn 15

> Our souls and bodies face our tasks. We stand no longer hopeless.
> A thousand sacrifices purged and newly shaped our people.
> Those who through death have trodden, now stand within our ranks.
> To heroes' deeds they beckon; Lord, give us endless power.

The Charge to the Congregation:

> Brother, comrade, listen, gaze in your inmost heart!
> Lives yet your father's mood within that blood's dear shrine?

> Our folk can still enjoy a valor strong and true,
> E'en though the foe can mow our lives as falls the grass.

> Dark death disjoins the frame and shuts our eyes to light.
> Yet brave hearts in our folk—they die and wither not.

> They breathe from sources deep, they grow from wholesome roots,
> And to their grandsons flows the valor of their blood.

> So stand, who'er it be, before God straight and proud,
> And to the banner stand, in holy willingness.

(*Announcements*)

The Congregation Sings:

> Tune: "Valet will ich dir geben"
> We stride on side by side, fresh 'wakened to our tasks
> Though hell should with us strive, in God's own power we stand.
> We struggle, and we spy the banner in the dawn.
> No storm or death's dark dread disjoins our settled faith.

ADORATION

Prayer.

A peal of bells for prayer

We remember in honor the dead, the heroes, who died in the storms of war and in the battle for the young Reich—the offering of work—the dead, who went from us into the peace of the homeland! They died—they live!

Threefold toll of bells

We remember the mothers and the children whom they bore.
Lord, bless them and preserve them steadfast in thy people;
And be with all who endure suffering and misfortune.
Lord, summon our hearts to helpful, saving deeds!

Threefold toll of bells

We remember the Germans in all the world. Lord, endue them with honor and life, and strengthen in them and in all of us the German conscience.
Preserve the Führer and our people and Reich!

Threefold peal of bells

Our Father, who art in heaven . . . .

The Congregation Sings: Hymn 7

Father, we leave thee not. Our home and peace art thou.
Eternal life below, our stay when all betray.
Regally, we thee entreat, Germany's weal we ask of thee.
Father, we leave thee not!

Benediction:

Lord, accompany us!
Lord, show us thy grace!
Lord, give us peace!

Hymn of the Congregation: Hymn 13

We are thousands and yet one, in the faith on which we're founded.
Earth and heaven, bind us in one, that we nevermore shall perish,
Proudly in all tempests stand!

We are thousands and yet one, in the loyalty that binds us,
Heart to heart by love inflamed, 'til the stars in splendor rise
And we pass to those who've died.[1]

[1] From the hymnal of the German Christians, *Gott mit uns! Hilfen zur Feiergestaltung* (Weimar: Verlag Deutsche Christen, 1939), pp. 13-16.

SELF-CRITICISM AND CONFESSION IN
COMMUNIST CHINA

Anyone who witnesses the big public sessions is conscious of an extraordinary perfection of method, an incomparable handling of crowds. Mass hysteria is deliberately created, it rises, and grows, until the depersonalized crowd is no more than the unconscious plaything of the leaders. When the meeting picks on someone for denunciation, a great wave of hatred is released; it is infused, distilled to a degree which becomes appalling. We know nothing more calculated to bewilder than the nocturnal meetings which, literally translated, are called "recital of the miseries of life." In the semi-darkness, in strained silence, each member of the actor-audience comes in turn to the middle of the circle and weeps at the recollection of his former existence and the misery and oppression of which he was the victim. The sinister lamentation sometimes swells as the shrill voices of women, and the cries for vengeance against those responsible for all the many evils of life rise in intensity. The lowest and most frightening depths are reached when one of the accusers points to the father, mother, wife, or child of one of those present. Then, indeed, one is conscious of the diabolical character of this evil thing.

Stranger still, if it were possible, are the weekly confessions of soldiers. Each must confess, before the assembled company, the number of times he has betrayed the Communist ideal and include even his most secret personal failings. In the course of such a public confession one can see the guilty man sob and even roll himself on the ground in despair. During the long "retreats" the whole of those attending must confess like this in greater detail and the confession ranges over the whole of life in all its activities, including even the most intimate secrets of family or conjugal life. The atmosphere of these assemblies cannot be described; one must have experienced it for oneself. The victims in the end arrive at the firm conviction that the Communists know all, that they read the very thoughts of the penitent, that there is nothing for it but to confess completely to absolutely everything.

The most extraordinary ceremony of all is perhaps that at which young soldiers pledge themselves body and soul, to the Communist cause. The church is draped in black, and here and there are symbols of mourning. The soldiers, in grim silence, enter one by one and take up their positions without making the slightest noise. First comes a discourse by the commissar in a low voice, dull and monotonous; it consists of an enumeration of all the errors of thought and action of which these poor wretches have been guilty. Everything possible is done to play on the emotions. Soon the atmosphere becomes unbearable. Another orator, and yet another, follows the first: the tension rises. A soldier bursts into sobs, another and another. In a few minutes everyone is weeping and groaning. The meeting is then adjourned and each one retires to meditate and to bewail the terrible system of which he had been a victim since birth, and his ancestors before him. For a couple of hours, all over the presbytery, there are tears and lamentations.

The soldiers are reassembled; a different sort of meeting this time is held, at which the beauty and grandeur of the future life are extolled.

It starts all over again the next, and the following day, alternating between contrition and disillusion. Outside these "exercises" total silence is enforced, nothing must disturb the time set apart for solitary meditation. On the evening of the third day, each one takes solemnly, before the assembled company, the pledge to dedicate his life and blood to the triumph of the Communist ideal throughout the world; each puts himself at the service of humanity.[1]

[1] From Francis Dufay and D. A. Hyde, *Red Star versus the Cross* (London: Paternoster Press, 1954), pp. 111-13.

CULT OR CUSTOM?

Although in his speech on culture at the Party Congress in 1938 the Führer expressly stated that National Socialism does not represent a cultic movement, we still often encounter statements which speak of a "cultic deepening of festive forms," or "cultically-formed life festivals," "the new cult of our world-view," or similar statements.

For this reason it seems that some clarification is necessary. In the language of politics, cult is the form of expression for a religion—which is not born of nature-racial knowledge and views, but rather sets forth transmitted doctrine. Its cult makes use of mystical, charming agencies and magical actions. It seeks, through the good humor of an all-powerful God, to work abjectly and thankfully, appeasingly and imploringly. Cult is conducted by a mediator between man and the divine.

In our National Socialist understanding of life, on the other hand, we speak of "celebration," "festival," or "custom." In its symbols and symbolic action custom is the expression of a world-view and of a belief in fate based on racial principles. In custom our kind of man makes his profession to the fateful ordering of the world and thus to all of life; he engages in making his life, his kindred, and his community life an active part of the larger order; he seeks thereby to fulfill life's meaning and to arrive at continual renewal and rebirth.

The task of our custom and our celebration is therefore to give strength for the battle of life and existence. Our faith involves affirmation of the world.

The task of cult and of cultic celebration is, on the other hand, that of setting one free from this vale of tears and preparing for a supposedly better beyond. Religion, working behind this cult, involves contempt and cynicism regarding the world.

The relationship of our kind of man to the divine, to providence, to fate, is free, undogmatic, personal, and direct.

The religions of cult prescribe the "way to God" on well-worn paths and make use of professional mediation. They require dogma and liturgy.[1]　　　[signed:] *Str.*

[1] From *Idee und Tat.* Reprinted in Oskar Söhngen, *Säkularisierter Kultus,* pp. 61-2.

APPENDIX 6

BASIC CONSIDERATIONS FOR THE NATIONAL SOCIALIST LIFE FESTIVALS

The celebrations of the life-cycle will in the future bear the uniform designations:

Birth Festival

Marriage Festival

Festival for the Dead

They must be conducted in good form and solely in accordance with the world-view of National Socialism, which is called to regulate the entire life of the German people.

For that reason it belongs to the tasks of leadership and education through the National Socialist Movement that the Movement cooperate in the formation of all celebrations which are devoted to the reason and understanding of the participants. It must also direct its attention to the celebrations which are devoted to deepening the world-view of National Socialism through their effective operations on the feelings.

To these belong particularly the life festivals. All service organizations of the Party are for this reason obligated to cooperate in word and deed, to the extent of their competence, in the planning and execution of National Socialist life festivals.

The Führer's commissioner for the supervision of the entire spiritual and ideological training and education of the NSDAP is responsible for the form and content of the life festivals created by the Movement. In close cooperation with those service organizations of the Party responsible for the creation of the celebrations, he issues directions, directs the training and education, and carries out his work of supervision.

In earlier generations our people's life festivals were created by the clan. One of the most remarkable monuments of this kind of form created by Nordic humanity was the close union of the judicial process and the faith engendered by the race instinct. The reception of the traditional festivities bound up with the clan's beliefs required no special "personnel," no called intermediary, creator of the festival, or festival speaker. Rather the leader of the clan was the born preserver of its

193

customs, just as the Führer of the race or people filled this role at the celebrations of the larger fellowship.

With the introduction of Christianity, the church gradually took over the festive activities, while to clan- and folk-community there remained only the inherited social customs and feasting that went along with every festival. As a consequence of the church's exercise of control over the festivals, the clan-community became, in the course of centuries, unable to create life festivals of its own.

In more recent times the clan-community lost its cohesiveness through the spatial dispersal of its members and the attachment of community life to other circles of life. For this reason in its place stepped the family, which is further enlarged, by individual blood relations, into the kindred.

However, where a clan-community still exists under the leadership of the oldest man of the kindred, e.g., in the villages or smaller towns, he is to assist substantially in the creation of the life festivals of the Movement.

At the present time, many of the forms of life of the clan-community have passed over into comradeship in an organization or association. Thus the comradeship, too, will have its appropriate part in the formation of the celebration.

The state has made provisions, through its Registrar's Office, to register births and deaths in order to record population statistics for legal affairs, thereby giving members of the state the legitimation and protection of laws. Through the Registrar's Office the state handles marriages in the same way. Members of the Party, as well as others who, while believing in a divine ordering of the world, yet in their principles of life also profess the German community of blood and people, will wish to mark memorable days of the life-cycle in a festive manner within the circle of the family and the peoples' community.

From this there arises for the Party the task:

1. For adherents of the Movement, and for members of the people who deserve well of the Movement or who wish to participate in the Party, to take over the further planning and execution of their life festivals.

2. To develop National Socialist forms for life festivals which will later become customs for the German people.

Those festivals of birth, marriage, and death whose planning and execution is to be borne by the Party will be designated in these directives as "Life Festivals of the Movement." Simple weddings at the

Registrar's Office, or celebrations at the Registrar's Office at which a representative of the NSDAP merely takes part, are not to be counted as Life Festivals of the Movement.

Where Life Festivals of the Movement take place, the celebration at the Registrar's Office (as in the case of weddings, for example) is to be drawn in. Two separate celebrations, one of the Party and one at the Registrar's Office, are basically undesirable.

Exceptions are admissible particularly in view of the prevailing lack of appropriate space and the wartime encumbrance of the Registrar's Office.

Every mystical cult and every dark, magical action must be rejected in celebrations having the stamp of National Socialism.

"National Socialism is no cultic movement, but exclusively a peoples' political tenet which has grown out of racial knowledge" (Adolf Hitler in his speech on culture at the 1938 Party Congress).

The idea of a "Master of Festivals," a "dedication warden," or some similar official or unofficial personage commissioned exclusively and permanently for the conduct of the festivals, is to be sharply rejected.

If in the exercise of his office the Registrar participates in the registration celebration, he, too, must take care that his words and actions be concise and to the point.

Ceremonies involving speaking and honoring are capable of transmission; one can participate in them wherever he finds himself. But behind any action must be some power or idea; e.g., the state is behind the speech of the Registrar, the Movement is behind the Führer's word spoken by some ranking official.

Customs and actions must not derive their application simply from fashion. They are not merely to serve to render some fact visible. They must be firmly rooted in a world-view, in faith in an all-embracing world-order. The manner of a custom, the question of whether it has good form or is derived from some source, the question of whether the instruction was false—these are matters which the world-view finally decides.

In the course of German history many alien customs arising from alien powers were transformed and transmuted so that they could today become the unadulterated possession of the entire people. It is the task of National Socialist folklore to push through here the distinction between what is authentic and what is alien and to determine what values in the transmitted materials are viable for the people's work and their planning and execution of festivals.

Today ancient custom capable of life can still gain admittance to our festivals, and new forms will come into use which are capable of being handed on. However, the rediscovery of some ancient custom cannot lead to its convulsive revival. *Whatever is capable of life will be determined by the thought and action of the present and by its laws of life.* Every custom which is not understood or does not harmonize with time or place becomes painful and ridiculous.

The symbol, ranging from surroundings (e.g., a tree) to action (e.g., an exchange of rings), is—as in the case of a custom—the outgrowth of belief and world-view. For this reason no intellectual construction of some dark, senseless magic can take the place of the symbol. It belongs to the nature of the symbolic that it possesses a deep and clear, universally-binding and convincing content so that it need not be restlessly ladled out by intellectual or rhetorical devices. For this reason the "explication" of symbols or actions during the celebration is altogether superfluous.

In correspondence with the National Socialist world-view, the forms of our life festivals must be unpretentious and close to life. And they are not ceremonies designed for sentimental "edification." For this reason they must always have the character of being close to reality, full of life, and to the point. Celebrations which are simply fabricated are worse than none at all.

Our celebrations are not designed to provoke confessional [i.e., ecclesiastical] opposition. They should weld all elements of the people together. They should not attack other conceptions. Moreover, the celebrations must not become demonstrations against those who think differently.

Our celebrations are never superficial substitutes for ecclesiastical ceremonies.

The comparison of confessional celebrations with those of National Socialism and any utilization of ecclesiastical elements is to be avoided under all circumstances.

The ranking official or the person he commissions is accorded simply a "token of respect" in the conduct of any of the life festivals. . . . In addition to this, it is the task of the NSDAP and all members of the Party and people to help in the conduct of their festivals, as, e.g., to assist in the preparation and arrangement of suitable festival rooms, music, choruses, etc.

Most people still lack a number of the pre-requisites for the conduct of suitable celebrations:

of an external nature: common choral materials, incidental music, room decorations, festive clothing, etc.

of an internal nature: the certain sense of style for what is fit and unfit, for art and decoration, the sure feeling for what is appropriate and inappropriate.

These prerequisites, however, are to be created in the German people when the patterns of the foundations for these prerequisites have been established and implemented.

To achieve this is the task of National Socialist education. Previous difficulties can be overcome in the creation of a festival if there is clarity regarding the meaning and content of the festival.

In this connection attention is to be paid to

1. authenticity of the practices employed, and
2. authenticity of the feeling of all participants in the celebration.

One cannot render feelings visible, whether they are authentic or not. One cannot require of participants things which they are struggling against. For that reason simple verbal professions, loyalty oaths, and similar pathetic demonstrations are to be rejected.

From the various attempts of recent years certain forms of celebrations have already emerged which may be of value and validity for the future.

At one point the contemporary forms are to be distinguished especially from the old practice: in their capacity to be passed on to posterity. It would be false if we were to consider our life festivals as something *singular*. Birth, marriage, and death recur *eternally*.

For that reason these festivals must possess features which are capable of being handed on, which can become traditional, which live on in an unwritten form in the celebrating communities so that, quite of themselves, the celebrations become ever new and yet can be given form in their old significance.

For this reason nothing is more mistaken than to search for a new "sensation" in each celebration.

The capacity for transmission is, to a great extent, a question of planning and execution. Every form of celebration which cannot be handed down is, from the very outset, limited in its capacity to exercise a lasting effect upon people. Therefore little decisive importance can be attached to the extemporaneous talk or to the subjectively oriented speech or address; in practice, too, we recognize it more as a word of accompaniment for the action, as are watchwords and songs.

One can trace this fact back to the point that our piety is a piety of deed and that a beautiful speech signifies an experience, to be sure, but something which cannot be recaptured by anyone else. In any case, a speech cannot become a custom as such even should it, thanks to the gifts and tact of the speaker, be capable of conveying something personal.

Life festivals are not to be built up into great political affairs; care must be taken in particular that there be no division at the celebrations between "actors" and "spectators." Such misrepresentations often entice people to cover up their uncertainty in world-view by recourse to outward pomp or to mere artistic presentations (no theatrical productions).

In contrast to this, efforts are to be made that the celebrating community cooperate inwardly and actively in the celebration.

It is at this point, for example, that the need arises for a common treasury of songs for the entire people, which need not be introduced anew at each and every festival. . . .

National Socialist celebrations shall be:

Visible images of our world-view, living ingredients of the life community of our people, experiences which live on and work on in the celebrators. Celebrations shall call to life a faith in a world-order in which our people has its special rank and value.[1]

---

[1] From *Die Gestaltung der Lebensfeiern*, pp. 3-8.

ROUSSEAU ON CIVIL RELIGION

In the first ages of the world, men knew no kings but the gods, and no government but theocracy. They reasoned like Caligula, and their reasoning, at that time, was just. It requires the work of a very long period so to alter the sentiments and ideas of mankind as to make them acknowledge their fellow mortals for their masters, and flatter themselves that they will find their advantage in submitting to them.

From this single circumstance of there being a god placed at the head of every political society, it is evident that there were as many gods as peoples. Two peoples, strangers to each other, and almost always in a state of hostility, could not long continue to acknowledge the same master: two armies fighting against one another could not obey the same chief. Thus polytheism was the consequence of national divisions; and polytheism in turn gave rise to civil and religious intolerance, which are the same by nature, as I shall show hereafter.

The propensity which the Greeks indulged of discovering that it was their own deities who were worshiped even by barbarians sprung from that of regarding themselves as the natural sovereigns of those peoples. But in our days it is certainly a very ridiculous species of erudition that revolves around the question of the identity of the gods of different nations: as if Moloch, Saturn, and Chronos could be the same god! As if the Baal of the Phoenicians, the Zeus of the Greeks, and the Jupiter of the Latins could be the same! As if there could be something common to chimerical beings that have different names!

It may appear extraordinary that, in the days of paganism, when each State had its own cult and its own gods, there should have been no religious wars. The reason was that each State, having its peculiar cult as well as its own form of government, did not distinguish its gods from its laws. Political war was also theological; the jurisdiction of their gods being, as it were, limited by the boundaries of the nation. The gods of one country had no right over the people of another. The gods of the pagans were certainly not jealous gods; for they divided the empire of the world among themselves: even Moses and the Hebrews lent themselves to this idea sometimes in speaking of the God of Israel. They regarded, it is true, as nothing the gods of the Canaanites, a people proscribed and condemned to destruction, and whose country they were to possess; but see how these Hebrews spoke of the deities of the neighboring peoples whom they were forbidden to attack! "The possession of that which appertains to Chamos your god," said Jephthah to the Ammonites, "is it not lawfully yours? We possess, under the same title, the lands which our conquering God has acquired." This seems to me to be fully acknowledging a parity between the rights of Chamos and those of the God of Israel.

But when the Jews, after being subject to the kings of Babylon and, later, to those of Syria, obstinately refused to acknowledge any other god but their own, the refusal was regarded as rebellion against their conquerors and drew upon them the persecutions which we read of in their history, and which were unrepeated until the commencement of Christianity.

Every religion, therefore, being peculiarly united with the laws of the State which prescribed it, there was no way of converting a people but by enslaving them, nor were there any other missionaries but conquerors; and the obligation of exchanging one cult for another being a law imposed on the vanquished, men had to conquer before they began to convert. So far indeed were men from fighting for the gods, that it was the gods, as in Homer, that fought for the men; each party demanded victory from his own god and repaid him for it by additional altars. The Romans, before they took a place, summoned its gods to abandon it; and when they left the Tarentines with their angry deities, it was because they considered these deities as being already subjugated to their own and forced to do them homage. They indeed often left the people they had vanquished their gods, in the some manner that they left them their laws. A wreath presented to the Jupiter of the Capitol was frequently the only tribute they imposed.

Finally, the Romans having extended with their empire both their cult and their gods, and having often adopted those of the conquered by granting to both the right of the city, the peoples of that vast empire insensibly found themselves with a multitude of gods and cults, everywhere almost the same: and that is how paganism became, throughout the known world, one single religion.

While things were in this situation, Jesus came to establish a spiritual kingdom on earth, which, by separating the theological from the political system, made the State no longer one, and caused those intestine dissensions which have never ceased to agitate the Christian peoples. This novel idea of a kingdom of the other world could never have entered the heads of pagans, and they always considered the Christians as really rebels, who, with a hypocritical air of entire submission, were only seeking the opportunity of rendering themselves independent and masters by artfully usurping the authority which in their weakness they pretended to respect. This was the cause of the Christians being persecuted. . . .

But, leaving these political considerations, let us return to the subject of right, and lay down fixed principles on that important point. The right which the social compact gives the Sovereign over the subjects extends no further than is necessary for the public good. No Sovereign can therefore have a right to control the opinions of the subjects any further than as these opinions may affect the community. It is of consequence to the State that each of its citizens should have a religion which will dispose him to love his duties; but the dogmas of that religion interest neither the State nor its members except as far as they affect morality and those duties which he who professes them is required to discharge towards others. For the rest, every individual may entertain what opinions he pleases, without it pertaining to the Sovereign to take cognizance of them; for, having no jurisdiction in the other world, whatever the fate of its subjects in the life to come, it is not the Sovereign's business, provided they are good citizens in the present one.

There is therefore a purely civil profession of faith, the articles of which it is the business of the Sovereign to arrange, not precisely as dogmas of religion, but as sentiments of sociability without which it is impossible to be either a good citizen or a faithful subject. The Sovereign has no power by which it can oblige men to believe them, but it can banish from the State whoever does not believe them; not as an impious person, but as an unsociable one, who is incapable of sincerely loving the laws and justice, and of sacrificing, if occasion should require it, his life to his duty as a citizen. But if any one, after he has publicly subscribed to these dogmas, shall conduct himself as if he did not believe them, he is to be punished by death. He has committed the greatest of all crimes: he has lied in the face of the law.

The dogmas of civil religion ought to be simple, few in number, precisely fixed, and without explanation or comment. The existence of a powerful, wise, and benevolent Divinity, who foresees and provides the life to come, the happiness of the just, the punishment of the wicked, the sanctity of the social contract and the laws: these are its positive dogmas. Its negative dogmas I would confine to one—intolerance, which is only congenial to the cults we have excluded. . . .[1]

[1] From *The Social Contract,* translation revised and edited by Charles Frankel ("Hafner Library of Classics," Vol. I; New York: Hafner Publishing Co., 1949), pp. 115-17. Used by permission of the publisher.

EXTRACTS FROM THE SPEECH OF THE DEPUTY PREMIER, WALTER ULBRICHT, AT THE OPENING OF THE YOUTH DEDICATION YEAR IN SONNEBERG ON SEPTEMBER 29, 1957

Learning for Life—Learning for Socialism

My dear young men and women! . . . The working people and our youth strive toward the light of knowledge. Youth strives for a bright and happy future. We, your elders, have done everything possible to create a new life for our young people, a life free from capitalistic exploitation and suppression. But it is the task of youth now to cooperate in preparing further this path to Socialism's victory and to a happy life for our entire people. Brethren, onward to the sun, to freedom! In the German Democratic Republic the working class, in union with the working farmers and other circles of activists, has gained freedom, thanks to the heroic sacrifice of the Soviet people in the battle against Fascism. When we speak of freedom today we think of our brothers and sisters in Western Germany; for our greatest historic task consists in freeing the people of Western Germany, too, from militaristic suppression, from capitalistic exploitation and slavery through the forces of West German monopolistic capitalism and of NATO. That is the goal toward which we strive. It is this great goal, the happiness of our people under Socialism, that is served also by the Youth Sessions and the Youth Dedication, the preparation of our youth for entrance into adult life.

Interesting and Instructive Youth Sessions

Today we are celebrating the beginning of the Youth Sessions. In the months ahead veterans of work, who have taken part in the great struggles of the German working class, activists who have achieved successes in the contest for Socialism, scientists, artists, athletes, will speak to you, and you will learn in an interesting way how the working class has fought for over a century now against exploitation and suppression, for right, freedom, and prosperity, how the workers strug-

gle in our Socialist factories for higher production, how scientists pene-
trate the secrets of nature, how writers, playwrights, musicians, and
sculptors create new works, in order to beautify the life of our entire
people and in order to develop German culture further to become a
Socialist national culture.

A Tradition of the Workers' Movement

In recent years Youth Dedication has more and more become a festival of our Republic. The Youth Dedication is a fine old custom
which the Socialist workers' movement has continued. Youth Dedication was not introduced into the German Democratic Republic only in
recent years. In Western Germany, too, the children go to Youth Dedication. I personally took part in the Youth Sessions, in preparation for
Youth Dedication in Leipzig, from the fall of 1906 to Easter, 1907.
My mother told me it would be valuable for my later life if the step
into a new life, into the adult world, were to be prepared by participation in Youth Dedication. . . . You, dear young friends, will learn
about the laws governing the development of nature and society, in order that you may employ this knowledge in collaborating in the building of a finer life under Socialism. The formation of a new life of a
people, the building of Socialism, requires much knowledge. The person who becomes an efficient expert, who acquires a complete education, will live better and more happily.

Win All the Young!

For this reason we want every young man and woman who has
reached this age to take part in the Youth Sessions and Youth Dedication, since they would otherwise miss important elements of knowl-
ledge which they would be putting to use in later life. The workers'
class bears a heavy responsibility for encouraging a greater number of
our young men and women to take part in the Youth Dedication and
in making arrangements for it even more interesting. This is not simply a matter for the Commission on Youth Dedication but also for the
workers in our factories, for trade union leaders, for the Party organizations, and for the cultural divisions in the Councils. We older people
will not go on living forever; the young must carry the great task forward and to its goal. For that reason it is important, particularly in
the factories, to clarify the basic meaning of the Youth Dedication for
the workers and to convince them of the necessity of their children's
participation in Youth Dedication. This work of convincing will be

carried out most effectively where there are factory activists for Youth Dedication. For this reason it is advisable to form aggressive activists for Youth Dedication in all the factories, particularly also in the Machine and Tractor Stations, in the peoples' own Departments, and in the Agricultural Production Communities. They should, in closer cooperation with the Women's Committees in the factories, explain the social significance and the educational value of Youth Dedication. I would like to emphasize expressly that all young men and women should participate in the Youth Dedication, irrespective of whatever world-view their parents have or whatever the world-view in which they have been brought up. The Youth Sessions and the Youth Dedication serve the development of well-rounded people who are also strong in character.

Our Young People and Their Historic Task

My dear young friends! Ever since there has been exploitation and suppression in the world, the exploited and the suppressed have longed for freedom and a better life. . . . Socialism is the only order for free men within society, since the working class, in union with the working farmers and other working people, exercises political power, since the forces of peace rule, and since through the removal of exploitation of man by man they guarantee a happy future for all men. Since in the German Democratic Republic the workers themselves have the powers of state in their hands, and the development in social and cultural areas forges ahead in a Socialist sense, the German Democratic Republic has become the true Fatherland of the people, the Fatherland of its youth.

What You Learn, Why You Learn

. . . You know that among us the workers and farmers exercise the power. You, too, should work along and interest yourselves in political life. . . . Among us the truth is taught, and it is simpler than certain fanciful thinking. You should know by what natural means, for example, the planetary system, the earth, man, and all other forms of life arose. It was not supernatural forces that were at work there; rather, everything in the universe has its natural causes. Exert yourselves to appropriate this knowledge. Science is always penetrating further into the secrets of nature and is shedding light everywhere where there is still darkness. Later you will perhaps yourselves explore nature's laws and help in extending the light of knowledge. Whoever permits himself to be impeded today in learning the laws governing nature and society, in throwing overboard old, outlived dogmas, is thereby only injuring himself. Whoever does not love the light of knowledge will reap his own disadvantage. Distinguished intellectuals have led an energetic battle for the enlightenment of youth against outmoded conceptions which stood in the way of progress. The great civic humanist Johann Gottfried Herder himself said in his School Address in the year 1798: "A boy must explore the natural sciences and must study nature in order that he may enjoy life, that he may recognize and make proper use of the gifts of nature, so that finally the manifold superstitions and errors may disappear which have never made the human race happy and simply do not belong to our day. . . . Our time does not need the knowledge of words, but educated, useful, skillful men."

Learning to Recognize the Truth

The Youth Dedication helps you recognize the truth, to appropriate knowledge which you urgently need for later life. But there are people who are not pleased by this. That is why they agitate against the Youth Dedication and against our schools. For example, Pastor Suppes of Lieberwolkwitz near Leipzig made the children learn a "confession of faith" which he had invented and from which I quote: "I believe that God has created me and all creatures. Not what is taught in school, but what the pastor teaches is right." We are prepared to conduct a free exchange of views about this. But we ask: Is this what you call education of youth for free, independent thought when the young people are required in confirmation instruction to believe that they have been created by supernatural beings? We want youth to have the opportunity to become familiar with the discoveries of the most advanced learning. Our schools form part of the scientific arrangements of a Socialist state. . . .[1]

[1] From *Neues Deutschland*, October 1, 1957. Reprinted in U. Jeremias, *Die Jugendweihe in der Sowjetzone*, pp. 92-95.

EXCERPTS FROM THE COMMISSIONER'S ADDRESS AT THE NAME GIVING IN ALTENHEIM, THURINGIA, ON CHRISTMAS DAY, 1957

"The Socialist Name Giving is a confession to our workers' and farmers' state, the first Socialist German state. With the reception of Name Giving you stand in the ranks of fighters for peace, Socialism, and progress. . . .

"Take care, dear parents and dear relatives, that from earliest infancy these children are educated to become zealously conscious Socialist men. These children will experience not only the Socialist order of society, but the Communist as well. We must become their conscious molders; we must carry on Lenin's work. Here our state, too, will help them, a state which grants our children every loving care. They shall be able to develop according to their abilities. I want to admonish all of you assembled here to devote all your energies to the building of Socialism and the preservation of peace. It depends on your training whether these children will one day become worthy members of our new society. . . .

"Our children gaze into a happy future. . . ."

[Three children were received into the "Socialist community" on this occasion. A special room, similar to the sacristy of a church, had been prepared in the city clerk's office. The table of the Commissioner of Vital Statistics had been decorated with potted flowers and lighted candles. Behind him was the bust of Soviet Zone President Pieck, draped with flags of the German Democratic Republic. The ceremony began with Handel's "Largo." After his address the Commissioner of the Office of Vital Statistics handed the parents a savings account book of 100 German marks, the text of his address, and a certificate validating reception of the "Socialist Name Giving" for their children. As the parents left the city clerk's office with their children they were greeted at the door by Young Pioneers who presented them with several pots of flowers. The event was also entered in the family geneological record.][1]

[1] Excerpts and descriptive comment from *Vor der Jugendweihe die Sozialistische Taufe.*

SELECTED BIBLIOGRAPHY

SELECTED BIBLIOGRAPHY

Abrams, Ray H. *Preachers Present Arms.* Philadelphia: Round Table Press, 1933.

Almond, G. A. *The Appeals of Communism.* Princeton: Princeton University Press, 1954.

Arendt, Hannah. *The Origins of Totalitarianism.* New York: Harcourt, Brace and Co., 1951.

Arnold, Heinz, ed. *Die Jugendweihe in der Deutschen Demokratischen Republik.* Berlin: VEB Deutscher Zentralverlag, 1961.

Arnold, T. W. *The Symbols of Government.* New Haven: Yale University Press, 1935.

Aron, Raymond. *The Century of Total War.* Boston: Beacon Press, 1955.

Aulard, A. *Le Culte de la Raison et Le Culte de L'Être Suprême.* Paris: Felix Alcan, 1909.

Barbu, Zevedei. *Democracy and Dictatorship.* New York: Grove Press, 1956.

Baron, Salo Wittmayer. *Modern Nationalism and Religion.* New York: Harper and Brothers, 1947.

Bloethner, Hans. *Gott und Volk: Soldatisches Bekenntnis.* Berlin: Morus-Verlag, 1959.

Bocheński, Joseph M., and Niemeyer, Gerhart. *Handbuch des Weltkommunisus.* Freiberg-München: Karl Alber, 1958.

Buchheim, Hans. *Glaubenskrise im Dritten Reich.* Stuttgart: Deutsche Verlags-Anstalt, 1953.

Cineris, Karl. *Jugendweihe und ihre Hintergründe.* Würzburg: Echter-Verlag, 1956.

Crossman, Richard (ed). *The God That Failed.* New York: Bantam Books, 1952.

Dibelius, Otto. *Grenzen des Staates.* Tübingen: Furche-Verlag, 1949.

————. *Reden an eine gespaltene Stadt.* Stuttgart: Kreuz-Verlag, 1961.

Die katholische Kirche in Berlin und Mitteldeutschland. Berlin: Morus-Verlag, 1962.

Eliade, Mircea. *Myths, Dreams and Mysteries.* Translated by Philip Mairet. New York: Harper, 1960.

The Evangelical Church in Berlin and the Soviet Zone of Germany. Berlin: Eckart Verlag, n.d.

Franke, Uwe, ed. *Neue Menschen feiern auf neue Weise: Gedanken und Hinweise zu sozialistischen Lebensfeiern.* Magdeburg: Druckerei Volksstimme, n.d.

Friedrich, Carl J. (ed.). *Totalitariansm.* Cambridge: Harvard University Press, 1954.

Gabriel, Ralph. *The Course of American Democratic Thought: An Intellectual History since 1815.* New York: Ronald Press, 1940.

Greeley, Andrew. "Myths, Symbols and Rituals in the Modern World," *The Critic,* XX, 3 (Dec. 1961, Jan. 1962).

Guardini, Romano. *Der Heilbringer in Mythos, Offenbarung, und Politik.* Stuttgart: Deutsche Verlags-Anstalt, 1946.

Hauer, Wilhelm. *Germany's New Religion.* New York: Abingdon Press, 1937.

Herman, Stewart W. *It's Your Souls We Want.* New York: Harper and Brothers, 1943.

Hofer, Walter (ed), *Der Nationalsozialismus. Dokumente 1933-1945.* Frankfurt/Main: Fischer, 1957.

Hook, Sidney, *The Hero in History.* Boston: Beacon Press, 1955.

Immer, Karl. *Entchristlichung der Jugend. Eine Materialsammlung.* Wuppertal-Barmen: Verlag Unter dem Wort, 1936.

Jeremias, U. *Die Jugendweihe in der Sowjetzone.* Bonn: Bundesministerium für gesamtdeutsche Fragen, 1958.

Kulturspiegel der Sowjetzone. Issued by the Federal Republic of Germany, Bonn.

Kurz, Otto Ernst. *Kleines Elternbuch. Gespräche mit Eltern über Familienerziehung.* Berlin: Volk und Wissen Volkseigener Verlag, 1961.

Littell, Franklin H. *The Free Church.* Boston: Beacon Press, 1957.

Mannheim, Karl. *Ideology and Utopia.* New York: Harcourt, Brace, and Co., 1936.

Marty, Martin. *The New Shape of American Religion.* New York: Harper, 1959.

Mathiez, Albert. *Les Origines des Cultes Révolutionnaires.* Paris: Société Nouvelle, 1904.

Meinhold, Peter. *Caesar's or God's.* Minneapolis: Augsburg, 1962.

Miller, William Lee. *Piety Along the Potomac: Notes on Politics and Morals in the Fifties.* Boston: Houghton Mifflin, 1964.

Monnerot, Jules. *Sociology and Psychology of Communism.* Boston: Beacon Press, 1955.

Otto, Bertram. *Hitler marschiert in der Sowjetzone.* Bonn: Berto-Verlag, 1961.

Pressespiegel der Sowjetzone. Issued by the Federal Republic of Germany, Bonn.

Pseudosakrale Staatsakte in der Sowjetzone. Namensweihe, Jugendweihe, Eheweihe, Grabweihe. Bonn: Bundesministerium für gesamtdeutsche Fragen, 1959.

Schmidt, Kurt Dietrich, *Germanischer Glaube und Christentum.* Göttingen: Vandenhoeck & Ruprecht, 1948.

Söhngen, Oskar. *Säkularisierter Kultus.* Gütersloh: C. Bertelsmann Verlag, 1950.

Solberg, Richard W. *God and Caesar in East Germany.* New York: Macmillan, 1961.

Talmon, J. L. *The Origins of Totalitarian Democracy.* New York: Praeger, 1960.

Thomas, Ulrich. *Staatsallmacht und Ersatzreligion.* Munich: Schaefer-Verlag, 1961.

Voegelin, Erich. *Die politischen Religionen.* Stockholm: Bermann-Fischer Verlag, 1939.

Vor der Jugendweihe die sozialistiche Taufe. Bonn: Bundesministerium für gesamtdeutsche Fragen, n.d. (*ca.* 1958).

Warner, W. Lloyd. *The Family of God.* New Haven: Yale University Press, 1961.

————. *The Living and the Dead: A Study of the Symbolic Life of Americans.* New Haven: Yale University Press, 1959.

Wiederkehr, Emil. *Jugend im Bannkreis der roten Moral.* Bern: Hilfskomitee für die Opfer des Kommunismus, 1958.

Williams, J. Paul. *What Americans Believe and How They Worship.* New York: Harper and Brothers, 1952.

INDEX

INDEX

Type, 11 on 13 and 10 on 11 Garamond
Display, Garamond
Paper, G. M. Antique

DATE DUE